WHAT IS ENERGY?

A CALL TO THE SPIRITUAL CORE OF MAN

SAMPSON IRUOHA

UPBUILDING PUBLICATIONS
www.theupbuilding.com

For the Furtherance of Spiritual Development

ISBN: 978-0-9865906-0-3

Published by Upbuilding Publications Publishing Co.

www.theupbuilding.com

E-mail: admin@theupbuilding.com

Design by Iain Hamilton

THIS BOOK addresses the primary form of energy in Creation and the need for its right recognition and usage for the development of mankind and their surroundings. Over millennia this energy has been misdirected by man due to his ignorance of its existence and nature of working. As a consequence, only works that have led to despair, chaos and destruction have formed in great numbers and grown through the thinking and general activity of men. The right use of this energy always leads to upbuilding in Creation, because it brings together and holds forms and substances in ways that only encourage upward growth and beauty.

Loss of this energy, through non-recognition and lack of absorption and right use, leads to a decrease in its supply and in the effects of its magnetic and upbuilding power. Disintegration or "a falling apart" results from this lack of or reduction in the flow of the currents of this primary energy, and takes the form of the break-down in peace, morality and the general ability to experience true joy by mankind.

In this hour of twelve, when the fruits of the wrong use of this power are returning to man in earnest and with great force and rapidity, with the threat of destroying him and his world, it is paramount that its true nature becomes known to man, so that he may respond rightly to what comes to him in this time and avert the irreversible destructive and devastating fate that lies at the end of the path upon which he has treaded now for ages.

Energy is very easily associated with movement. Wherever the word "energy" is used it is invariably connected with movement or the capacity to achieve it. We experience its effects every moment in the course of our daily activities here on earth, in the various forms in which it manifests. As it travels from one form to another it produces effects that correspond to its nature and to the nature of the form transmitting it.

The way that it manifests from within a species or creature is an expression of the kind of energy the species or creature is able to absorb, because the species passes it on in corresponding form as it absorbs the energy. It reflects the nature of the energy-form that it absorbs in the course of its own activities, and thereby indicates the true nature of the activity.

One of the ways that energy is experienced, for instance, is in the way that it comes up from within us as human beings as we respond to the goings-on in our surroundings. It is very unlikely that a person could go from one moment to the next without experiencing a change or changes in the forms or intensities of the thoughts or pictures arising and fading away within him, transforming as they develop, or quickly disintegrating away due to lack of sustaining support. These thoughts and pictures are all energy-forms that have specific effects that accord with their individual natures.

Some of these energy-forms can, for instance, make one laugh, while others can move one to tears of sorrow. Some can induce the ignition of a raging flame of anger within a person, while others can have a mellowing effect which is able to neutralize or push back all dark emotions. In every case, however, the particular impression moves the one concerned towards the expression of a particular emotion. The impression is transformed within him into that particular emotion. The emotion thus produced or formed is the work of the one impacted by the energy-form. It is the effect of a particular kind of movement or vibration, and through this movement - which is the effect of energy - energy is transferred, transmitted or passed on. It is passed on into the form assumed by the emotion.

The producer of the emotion receives the impression that led to the emotion as an effect of a particular form of energy, and then transforms it to the emotion-form that he deeply feels as a consequence of the im- pression. The entity known as spirit, which animates man from within and causes him to move and respond to stimuli, is at the same time the living core of man; the *real man*.

It is the spirit that we recognise when we see man. Whatever is seen as coming from man is the effect of this entity that lives within him as his core, which in fact is the real man, and which needs and uses the physical body solely for the purpose of interacting with the physical environment of the earth. A corresponding effect of the vibration of this entity is transmitted to the physical surroundings of man through his physical body, and, conversely, the effects of physical energy-forms are transmitted to this entity – spirit – through the physical body. So, the physical body serves merely as a tool for the transmission of vibrations from the human spirit to the its physical environment, in which *it* is known as *man,* and from this physical environment back to the animating core, the spirit, and thus to the actual being.

The animating core within man, which requires the physical body as its tool, is known as spirit; it is a species of spirit. Spirit is energy. The energy that flows through Creation and brings about all the effects that man is able to experience is spiritual in nature, thus we experience in the happenings around us the effects of the movement of currents of spirit.

Outside of and above the World of Matter spirit has different forms, which depend on the frequency of the vibration or movement within the particular form of spirit. The ones with the highest frequency of vibration exist at the highest point in Creation, farthest away from the earth and the World of Matter to which the earth belongs, if one were to go upwards from here; while the ones with the lowest frequency of vibration form the lowest layer or plane in the gradations that make up the Spiritual part of Creation.

The "spiritual part" of Creation is referred to as such because it is purely spiritual, without any other species, such as the material species, being able to be there. Energy flows through Creation from the species of spirit with the highest frequency of vibration to the ones with the least degree of movement. In the process, it flows through all the intermediary forms of spirit in the spiritual part of Creation, which act as step-down transformers of the energy that eventually gets to the World of Matter and the earth. The energy currents that flow through the World of Matter, which includes the earth, are absorbed and passed on by those species of spirit with the lowest frequency of vibration, which reside and work in the World of Matter during the period of their development to greater consciousness and maturation.

This is akin to the flow of electrical currents from a point of high voltage to one of lower voltage, through a series of step-down points or transformers. At the endpoint of this process the right amount of voltage is delivered in a form that is not too much, but is just right for the end-user of the electrical power. The effect of the flow of electrical current is described as its power, and this power has to be just right for the individual points where it is consumed if it is to be made use of in the right way and not cause harm.

It is the same with the flow of spiritual currents, which bear the power that moves and maintains Creation. The entity at the core of man, the human spirit of earthman, is the lowest in the gradations of spirit that receive of this power. It transmits this power to its material surroundings through the nature of the energy-forms that it produces or forms in response to what impresses upon it.

What determines the nature of the product of this transformation and transmission process is the existing nature or degree of maturity of the human spirit in question, prior to its being impacted by the impression to which it then responds. In fact, the nature of the impression itself, which is drawn out of a happening by the human spirit concerned here, is dependent upon the existing nature of the human spirit prior to its being confronted with the happening. It is this nature that determines how the happening impacts it. This is because it is this nature that determines what the human spirit *attracts* from the happening as an impression. So, a person can perceive disappointment or justice depending on how he has developed inwardly prior to the happening that prompts a response from him.

The nature of the human spirit is therefore responsible for everything that comes to it as a man on earth; be it in the form of the thoughts that come to him, the deep inner feelings that give rise to these thoughts, or in the forms of the words and the actions directed at him from others. It is in this way that it determines what it experiences. It expresses through this process what it wishes to experience, whether or not it is aware of it. In this ability to decide what it wants to experience, by the way it attunes itself, lies the freewill of the human spirit.

If it did not have this ability to decide, that is, if what came to it was not dependent on some criteria that it had control over, then there would be no boundaries set to what it could attract to itself with its inherent ability to attract. It would then draw to itself all manner of things, including things that are beneficial to its development as well as things that are not. It would also draw to itself many a thing that it would lack the capacity to deal with, and would end up being perpetually burdened and unable to rise upwards for its true task in Creation.

As it is, however, man only attracts that which conforms to his inner attitude, and because he has the capacity to form what he attracts, he also has the capacity to rightly deal with all the consequences of it, favourable or unfavourable. If the volition or deep desire is able to come from him, then he is also able to form it aright. If it were not possible for him to form it aright, then he would not have been able to form it even wrongly; he would not have had the opportunity to engage it in the first place. So, what determines how he deals with what comes to him is his inner nature, his inner attitude. This also allows him to recognise what has been formed wrongly, through the way it impacts him, and makes it possible also for him to set it right in his response to the impact. It gives him the opportunity to know or taste of this kind of impact, and to steer his volition or deep inner desiring in a different direction.

What a particular producer of form feels in his automatic reaction to a particular happening will be different from what the next person will feel upon experiencing the same happening. In order words, both persons will form different *works* in reaction to a particular happening, and thus produce different effects for others to experience and react to. That which they produce is their responsibility, their own work. It shows how they have received what has been passed on from above them as radiation, as streams of energy particles, and what they make available to others in the process of transmitting this radiation. That which is transmitted is either dimmed through being distorted, or is kept pure and bright through clear transmission.

The human spirit forms what it experiences by attracting to itself the conditions that make possible the manifestation of the experience. When it is moved to vibrate in a particular way, a form of energy is generated in its surroundings, which then goes on to transmit effects that correspond to this deep emotion, *spiritual perception* or *intuitive feeling*. In this way the human spirit passes on to its surroundings effects that are similar to what it feels or what it resonates with. If this vibration is a light one, beautiful and harmonious effects are generated; but if it is one of a low and burdensome nature, such as one of envy or of fear, then it will lead to those conditions that provide fertile soil for the rousing of envious emotions, and for the spreading of similarly weighted emotions such as distrust, greed, narrow-mindedness, discord, disharmony and chaos.

So, the effect of the spiritual on the material substance causes it to come together in ways that correspond to the vibration of the spirit, leading the development of matter in a direction determined by the nature of the spiritual volition of mankind. In this way, a particular kind of energy or other is transmitted to matter, which, itself (matter), cannot move without such movement-inducing effects of the spirit.

What is spiritually pure is attracted upwards to the origin of the spiritual currents, because it vibrates or moves in a similar manner to what exists in the Spiritual Realm above. The nature of the vibration determines the kind and amount of energy it absorbs and transmits. The purer the vibration, the closer it resembles and moves like what is in the higher Spiritual World or Plane, and the more spiritual substance it attracts or absorbs through this homogeneity or closeness. The flow of spiritual currents leads to the effect of magnetism among a definite species of substance within a definite range. This is because by its very nature everything spiritual attracts. It is, in fact, the attractive effect of the spiritual substance that leads to the movements that we are able to experience in different forms here on earth in the World of Matter.

The flow of spiritual currents brings about an effect that is similar to the magnetic field around a wire through which electricity is passed. The greater the current passed through the wire, that is, the faster the flow of electricity through the wire, the greater the generated magnetic field and magnetic or attractive power. Similarly, the greater the amount of spiritual substance that flows through a human being, the greater his attractive capacity and his ability to penetrate the material world around him; also, the greater the sphere of his influence in matter, which results from the magnetic pull upon material substance in a manner specific to his nature. Naturally, the higher one rises in his spiritual maturity and knowledge, the more his nature will reflect the purity that exists in the spiritual spheres above, and so the more purely-spiritual-currents he will draw to himself for transmission.

So, added strength and power come only through increased inner purity. This is because the currents that flow will have, due to their relative purity, the capacity to penetrate more deeply into matter and also more widely within it, and, through the process of attraction, have a greater formative influence on it. Such deep penetration always goes together with a considerable and corresponding breadth of influence, because the attractive influence reaches far in all directions, vertically and horizontally. What the one who possesses this power or ability produces will therefore correspondingly reflect, in an earthly or material way, the beauty and perfection of the Spiritual Realm. Thus, man cannot attain to such spiritual abilities and thus to such power without first purifying himself from within.

Here, the attainment to higher spiritual power or capability is merely the allowance of the flow of more spiritual currents than was previously the case for the individual concerned. The hindrance to this flow by man is brought about through his narrow-mindedness and one-sidedness; through his insistence on doing things only according to what he can see with his *present* limited capacity to perceive, which derives from his non-recognition, his disregard of and refusal to act on evidence that points to the existence of better and more efficient ways of acting; thus his incapacity for upward development. Such better and more efficient ways are only perceptible to the one who expresses the wish to see them, through being genuinely inwardly open to *attractive* guidance from above.

What is dense or impure sinks to low depths where the vibrations are slower and where what is formed is correspondingly less perfect and uglier, in both its appearance and in its feel to the human spirit. The range of influence of the one concerned is also correspondingly limited, just like a person on the first floor of a building sees much less of the surroundings of the building than one who stands on the twentieth floor. The vantage point of the one who stands spiritually higher allows him to see more, and thus to have a greater influence through being able to impact and also interact with a wider area.

The capacity to rise so high lies in the capacity to move and to attract the required strength for it in the form of the flow of spiritual currents, which could then be transmitted to all that lies within such a wide perceptive range. The one concerned would have to be attracted or drawn upwards as he transforms himself to become more like what lies above. This is what allows him to reach to those heights from which he is able to draw more currents of spirit than he was able to prior to his transformation.

★   ★   ★

The residual currents of spiritual particles, which flow downwards as energy currents, attract to themselves the finest substances of matter as they descend downwards and make contact with the boundary where the World of Matter begins. At this boundary exists the finest and lightest species of material substance.

These particles of spirit, which lose intensity of movement as they move further away from the Source – because they increasingly lose movement-inducing warmth the farther they drift from the Source of Animation – become cloaked in the material substance that they have *naturally* attracted. The attraction of the material substance to the spirit particle leads to an aggregation of material substance that was formerly loose, and to the sinking of this newly-shaped form or aggregation due to increase in density.

The attraction of material substance, and the consequent development of forms in matter, occur because the spirit particle first passes through a plane in which an animating substance first forms a cloak around it. In other words the spirit particles first interact with a species of Creation the nature of which leads to the animation of matter. It is this animating substance, which possesses a formative nature, that then makes direct contact with matter, weaving it into a form that agrees with the urge within the spirit particle.

The attraction of loosely-existing fine material substance to the spirit particle leads to the formation of something denser, something more focused, because these formerly loose material substances come closer together around the attractive, vibrating spirit particle, with the animistic species forming the bridge. This phenomenon has been mainly experienced by men in its outermost forms, without their being able to see the finer, and thus, deeper preceding happenings.

Also, as a consequence of the cloaking, the emanations from the spirit particles, that is, the force of attraction which they naturally exert, become transformed, bringing about a different kind of vibration from the original (which existed in the uncloaked and pure spirit particle). This change in the vibration makes it possible for the next lower and denser substance of matter to be affected by the now changed power of attraction from the spirit particle (the World of Matter being composed of many planes, the coarsest and densest of which are the most tangible and visible to us as earthmen).

The transformation of vibration, due to the cloaking, serves as a bridge and a means for the transmission of energy from the spirit particle to this denser material substance, which would have remained alien to the spirit particle, with its specific kind of vibration, and, therefore, untouchable by it. It would not have been able to impact it had it not been for the transformation provided by the cloaking effect of the attracted finer and first layer of material substance. The attraction of the finer material substance would also not have occurred had the cloaking of the spirit particle by the attracted animistic substance not taken place before hand. So, each cloaking of the spirit particle brings about a transformation of the radiation and the possibility for the attraction of the next species of substance lower in the order of Creation. The new vibration comes closer to what the lower and denser material substance can relate to and respond to; hence the possibility of an attraction, of interaction.

So, the cloaked spirit particles sink further downwards, through becoming denser as a result of the coming together or aggregation into forms composed of the material substances, which they draw to themselves in the course of their descent. The gravitational pull, however, acts on the material substances and only pulls along the spirit particle – which is not subject to this gravitational pull – because it is indirectly bound, through the process described above, to the material substances.

In this way, the excess spiritual currents, or further effects resulting from the activities of spiritual beings in higher realms, sink to the regions of matter, bearing within them a correspondingly reduced impetus towards movement and development, compared to such as exists in the spiritual worlds above. As they pass through the various planes between the Spiritual World and the earth, they go on to form combinations through being attracted to one another. What is formed in the various planes are reflections in those planes of what has already formed in the planes of the Spiritual World, and they give expression to the nature of the vibrations within the human spirits living and working on those material planes. They give expression to the volitions of these spiritual beings, which magnetically hold the developing forms in their various shapes and kinds.

Here on earth, these particles become detectable as the subatomic particles, the electrons, protons, neutrons, atoms, etc., which scientists have been able to identify and study to some degree. It is in these basic forms, or through their effects, that earthmen have been able to detect the existence of the vibrating spirit particles. It is also at such early levels of development that the human spirits on earth influence, with their volition, the developments here on earth. But if men were to develop stronger equipment with which they could see even smaller particles, they would discover more worlds which today still remain unknown to them. There will be no end to discoveries of this kind, which could be made as man improves upon the existing equipment at any given time.

As man develops rightly in his material surroundings, he will also develop increased capacities of perception. Where the increased capacity to develop more powerful physical tools has led to his being able to see worlds that were formerly invisible to him, it would be because he has developed to the point of being able to see such worlds, even if they still lie within the gross material, physical world. His ability to develop and make use of such tools makes it possible for him to see such previously invisible worlds.

He brings this process to an end, however, or greatly reduces its potential when he makes his development a one-sided one. That is, one that cuts him off from the energy needed for his *inner* maturity and for all movement in Creation. This is because his advancements in the fields of science and technology will surpass that of his spiritual maturity, which is needed in the right form for his surroundings to develop in the right direction. He will therefore destroy his surroundings before he is able to make the best use of his physical discoveries. They will not bring *him* any benefit because they will be at the mercy of a weak spirit, which is unable to build upwards. All that will be built in this condition will lead downwards and to chaos and destruction.

But more about this later. Man, therefore, will continually discover worlds which were previously invisible to him the more powerful the tools he uses for this purpose become. And where, in this regard, he discovers movement, there he has seen an even earlier manifestation of the vibration of the cloaked spirit particles before the coming-together of what he may be able to see at the time. In other words, he will go well beyond the level of atoms and electrons the more he is able to see using more powerful equipment. Everything that he is able to discover, however, will always follow the Laws of Nature such as have been seen in the behavior of atoms, electrons and so on. This is because the animating particle cannot follow any other Law but that which governs all Creation.

The relatively weak vibrations of these cloaked spirit particles express the immense distance of the particles from their origin, and lead to combinations between them, which form the basic building blocks of the material worlds. These building blocks, in following the inherent urge towards development, which lies in all that is spiritual, and which is faintly reflected also in the vibrations of the sunken particles, strive towards union and development, which is the result of friction due to movement, according to the degree to which this can be achieved while within the species of matter in question.

In other words, they strive towards the formation of corresponding copies of what exists in the higher and more beautiful spheres, where movement is more rapid and the heat produced through friction more intense, making life there more aflame. The attractive force that comes from the stronger spiritual beings above pulls on them and maintains within them that vibrating movement that is the effect of spiritual attraction. In response to the inherent spiritual urge to develop, these spirit particles, with their particular kinds of vibration, attract one another according to homogeneity or relatedness, and grow into forms and shapes, which continue to develop and build upwards, to become coarser reflections of what already exist in the highest part of Creation.

This leads to the formation and development of the mountains, the streams, the forests and all the vegetation, in fact, everything in higher material spheres that corresponds to what we refer to here on earth as Nature. The same thing also takes place in this gross material plane where the earth is. Here also, all formations strive towards expressing in corresponding form what has already taken on form in higher regions. The celestial bodies, planetary and solar systems also form through the combinations of these cloaked particles, as far-flung secondary effects of a spiritual volition that took on form in the highest part of Creation; in the realm of more powerful spiritual beings, which have the capacity to receive and pass on greater amounts of spiritual currents with greater attractive and formative effects.

The species of Creation that is responsible for forming the bridge between the human spirit and matter is that to which the so-called Nature beings belong. It is they who form the bridge between the spiritual and the material in all matters. They are the animistic beings whose plane of origin (mentioned above) all that is spiritual must pass through prior to reaching and making contact with material substance. They carry out the forming in response to the attractive volition of that which is spiritual.

This happening (spiritual forming through the activity of the animistic beings) takes place on every layer or plane of matter through which the spirit particles pass in the course of sinking downwards. It is through this that worlds form in all those planes, expressing varying degrees of beauty and perfection, depending on how close the plane in question is to the Source of Power and Animation, to the Primordial Light, to God. The closer the species is to the Origin, the more perfectly and beautifully it forms itself and its surroundings.

The more the forms in matter develop for the better, the more power they absorb from Creation, since this power is needed for that necessary movement that leads to the generation of friction and warmth, which are needed for the generation of forms. As they develop thus the vibrations within the particles also change. They change to something stronger, higher and better, striving towards the spiritual species above. As this happens, the developing particles, with their now higher frequency of vibration, become even more subject to the attractive influence from the spiritual above, being at this point even more similar to them, and thus become drawn even further upwards through this increased attraction.

This pull upwards further increases the animation of the vibrating spirit particles at the core of the basic building blocks of matter, leading to the generation of different vibrations, and to a striving towards even more beautiful and more perfect combinations and forms; a trend that is directed upwards.

The attraction of the spiritual above acts, therefore, upon the spirit particles, and not upon the material substance, which is of an alien nature to the spirit. It is the upward-tending change in the vibration of the spirit particles, due to the increased energy transmitted through the attractive influence of the stronger spiritual species above, which leads to the formation of more beautiful material forms. This is because an improvement in the frequency of the vibration of the spirit particles leads to an improvement in their state and in how these cloaked basic units combine, and in what comes together or develops as a result of the combinations. The combinations are therefore dependent on the nature of the vibrations. Vibrations of a higher and purer nature lead to nobler and more perfect forms, while weaker and denser vibrations lead to more distorted and imperfect forms. Purity in this case refers to the degree to which the spiritual vibration is unhindered or undimmed through being passed or transmitted through the alien material cloaks.

That particle or species of spirit that is in the Spiritual Realm due to the nature of its vibration, which is dependent on its purity, cannot have any impurities on it. In this condition it vibrates without any dimming or difference from the kind that exists in its surroundings in the

Spiritual Realm. It is the similarity in the vibration that brings about the attraction to and the existence within the same plane.

The earth, where we currently reside, finds itself between the regions of Light and the regions of darkness. It is at the same time under the influence of the gravitational pull of the dense material substance, as it is under the influence of the higher spiritual. The way it develops or forms depends on the direction determined through the inner nature of men. When decisions or inner attitudes are formed due to reasons of a low, narrow or earthly nature, then the vibrations that determine the nature of the forms are correspondingly low, dark and narrow. They are sluggish and dull and produce forms that are correspondingly ugly, which come together in ways that express their lack of symmetry and balance, their lack of simplicity and beauty.

When the reason for the decisions or attitudes are high and light, then what is formed in matter is beautiful and vibrant, in accordance with the nature of the higher vibration to which the affected and corresponding spirit particles are attuned. The vibration of that which is formed expresses the nature of the vibrations of the basic units that come together for such a formation. The reverberations or effects of the movements of this form transmit this higher and lighter vibration to the surrounding material environment, so that this environment also forms itself beautifully, as it comes together under the attractive influence of the well-put-together light form.

To achieve the goal of nobler combinations and finer forms, the old forms have to fall apart, back to their basic units or building blocks, in order for something new to form in light of the new kind of vibration resulting from increased animation of the spirit particles, which drive the material substance and move it. For this reason we have in matter the continual and eternal process of development that goes from the sowing of seed to development and maturation, to the flowering and bearing of fruit, and finally to disintegration back to the basic units for the purpose of a reformation in a more beautiful way. This can be seen in the development of all forms observable in matter, including the stars, celestial bodies, plants, the bodies of men and animals, etc. It is also true for the material conditions of the developing human spirit, or, more specifically, the ways in which man experiences his conditions here on earth and in the broader World of Matter.

In a normal developmental process, when the old forms break down again in disintegration, more developed or changed spirit particles (still cloaked in material substance) are released as energy, and are attracted upwards due to the change in an upward direction. In their new states these particles can then contribute to the development and ennoblement of the material planes to which they still remain bound due to their still existing material coverings. The released energy *must* give expression to the volition or vibration that led to the formation of that which, in developing, comes to the point of disintegration for the purpose of reformation. So, the nature of what goes back into the corresponding environment is dependent upon what was fed into the developing form, that is, what was planted as seed in it which must later mature as fruit.

Some, which rise into finer material planes, because they descended through such planes on their way down to earth, return with new energy, and contribute to the formation of new environments as a consequence of their newly acquired vibrations, while those that remain on earth go on to form nobler forms as a result of the same happening.

In this way, the World of Matter was to develop and in fact did develop for a time, through a process that has been partly recognized and termed *evolution*, until a point was reached when the beings (also known as Nature Beings and previously visible to men of olden times, who often worshipped them) responsible for putting the forms together in matter could no longer build upwards without more spiritual (creative, motivating) currents from above. This could only be made available to them through spiritual beings, which alone have the capacity to attract and transmit the needed creative spiritual currents from above; this being possible because of their homogeneous spiritual origin, their Paradise.

At the same time as this point of potential stagnation and retrogression was reached, that is, when those beings responsible for putting together forms in the course of development came into need for a stronger motivational force than what was available, there were spirit seed-germs which were unconscious in the lowest part of the Spiritual Realm, and within which the urge to develop self-consciousness had awakened. These had to descend to the lower, slower regions of matter for the process of schooling in the workings of the Laws that govern all happenings in Creation, and gradually to develop through becoming more animated, spiritually stronger and brighter. They were to follow a path similar to that of the spirit particles, but they were much more than spirit particles, for they were to develop into self-conscious spiritual beings.

They were to work in matter and develop to maturity as they drew down for this purpose the necessary spiritual currents from the Spiritual Realm. Inevitably their material surroundings would benefit also from this since the presence of developing spiritual beings in matter would also mean the presence of a strong and increasing attractive force. Their upward-tending activities and natures would bring the strong spiritual currents above in the spiritual world even closer to the vibrating particles, which animate the material substance. The more of this current is drawn downwards from above, the better the material world would develop, because the increased animation within the spirit particles in matter, brought about through the increase in attractive power of the upward-developing spiritual beings, would lead naturally to the formation of better, more beautiful and more ennobled forms. Through these nobler forms would then pass more freely the lighter vibrations which only lead upwards.

★   ★   ★

Man draws energy when he forms his deep inner feelings, his thoughts, his words and his physically visible deeds. These are his works. The nature of his works is determined by his inner attitude, the nature of his inner desiring, his spiritual volition. This spiritual volition first manifests as his intuitive perception, as the expression of the perception of his spirit. The perceptions of the spirit are expressed in the form of vibrations, which shape themselves according to the natures of the perceptions. They give expression to how well the spirit is able to see and recognize the guiding rays of power which issue from out of Creation, from God.

The human spirit within whom exists the vibration to put into deed the Will of the Light, Which he has gleaned through his steadfast efforts, will produce those forms that make the perception of this Will more easily attainable. Such forms or works of the human spirit in question will have the effect of seeking to attract from within his fellow man the inner yearning for what is purer and higher. This, in the reciprocal effect of the sowing of the seed, can then lead the one concerned to the experiencing of corresponding conditions, which help him awaken to greater consciousness, awareness and true joy. The opposite is the case with those works that are born of a carefree attitude towards one's existence and the responsibilities attached to the unfolding of the promise that lies in it. Such would have the effects of encouraging man to glaze over everything, without allowing for beneficial inner reflections, which usually go with battles against old and narrow conceptions.

If the human spirit in man has buried his perceptive capacity too deeply in material substance, thus hindering his ability to see clearly the spiritual lessons and pictures in the happenings around him, he will respond to them in ways that will express or reveal this incapacity or limitation. With his responses he will initiate the development of energy-forms that will correspond to the basic nature of such responses, and thus of his current inner nature or state of maturity. These energy-forms give expression to the nature of the vibrations from him in response to what he has encountered.

For instance, a man could feel envy rise from deep within him when he learns of his friend's promotion at his place of work, while he (the envious one) may be struggling just to feed his family and himself.

The feeling of envy rises because of the way he views the situation. Perhaps his conception of success is limited to his ability to live comfortably without any struggles or hardships, while at the same time amassing material wealth. He may not see any spiritual benefit in the difficult conditions that may have developed for him to live through, because his focus is mainly on what is earthly and what brings earthly benefit and comfort. The news of his friend's promotion reminds him of some of the widely accepted earthly markers of success which he has not yet been able to attain, and this causes him to focus on what his friend possesses, and to wish to possess that for himself. He does not see the justice in this condition.

The one-sided view of the situation keeps him from seeing how his own specific condition could help him in his own spiritual development, in a way that would have been hindered by the possession of just that which he may have his envious eye on. So, the one-sidedness of his perception leads to the generation of such effects as cause him to maintain a narrow and one-sided vision. The form that develops as a consequence of this perception is ugly, just as one would expect envy to be and feel.

A person who has made the effort to experience the process of cause and effect, as it brings to him the consequences of his past inner volition, his thoughts and his actions, and who strives to always see the core of every happening, that is, the spiritual lesson for him in that which comes along his earthly path for his experiencing, will stay open through this process to a more complete picture of every happening than would be available to one who has not made this effort, who therefore keeps himself closed to a broader picture, and who simply takes in the happening superficially.

This kind of deepened view allows him to see that there is a reason behind that which materializes for him in his every earthly condition. He is able to see that it is not a random happening that gives to this or that person this or that kind of fruit, without rhyme or reason. Thus he is able to sense some justice in all happenings, which allows him to develop the trust that things must also change as soon as the starting point of the conditions that materialize for him, that is, his innermost desiring, changes for what is good and remains steadfastly on that path of goodness. That just as surely as his past spiritual indolence and associated ignorance led to his sowing those seeds that developed into dark and unfavourable conditions as their fruits, his conscious efforts to maintain a volition for what is good, and to live according to this volition in his thoughts, words and visible actions, must lead to an all-embracing good fruit.

Whatever then comes along his path while he steadfastly maintains this attitude and acts accordingly, must aid in his being able to see more clearly the right linkages between cause and effect, as well as see how he must act in order to bring about only what is good. The recognitions that will come to him along this path must lift him up inwardly and bring him true joy, liberation from the pressure of a lack of understanding. This is so, even if the conditions that he has to live through at first feel or appear unfavourable.

Only the *personal experiencing* of cause and effect, as it brings to man the conditions he has to experience, can allow him to experience this happening in such as a way as leaves a real and lasting impression with him, as a part of his inner make-up. Through this new inner make-up he sees the world around him differently, more clearly, with less dimming and distortion, i.e., more as it really is and less veiled by his wrongly formed conceptions and emotions. He is able to see beyond certain possible and often feared earthly implications of physical happenings, and to recognise their spiritual, and thus, broader effects, which, when made use of in the right way, cannot but lead to earthly conditions that are favourable in every way, and also in ways previously unimaginable to the one concerned.

This is because when man's gaze is only on what is earthly in the happening that presents itself to him, he also views it mainly with re-spect to how it impacts or could potentially impact his earthly condi-tion. He analyses with his earth-bound intellect how this fits with the conceptions he has formed up till then about what it will take to be happy. This all happens as if automatically, instantaneously. But it always happens in accordance with how the one in question has developed his perceptive capacity up to the time of the happening.

Such a person, who bases his judgement of the nature of a happen-ing on how (in his view) it impacts earth-life only, also must develop for himself a narrow range of possibilities for being happy, because such a narrow view, which permits him to see only the earthly perspective, also keeps him from seeing a wider range of possibilities for experienc-ing happiness. It is a mark of narrow-mindedness, which grows out of and is a part of one-sidedness; that one-sidedness which expresses itself in his inability to see beyond the earthly circumstance or form, thus the earthly side of it, and which consequently keeps his perception low and narrow.

It is because of this narrowness that the apparent good fortune of his friend causes envious intuitive feelings and thoughts to arise within him. With a broader view that comes from the personal and deeper experiencing of cause and effect, he is able to see the happening in an entirely different context, leading to an entirely different reaction or response from him, such as will lead to the generation of entirely different energy-forms, and the associated drawing of entirely different energy currents to himself for transmission to his surroundings.

The feeling of envy is an expression of a limited perception, which allows for the drawing of low and dense energy currents, and for the formation of distorted and ugly pictures and forms, such as those of envy, greed and fear. The distorted nature of the forms developed as a result will also make itself felt in corresponding ways by those concerned.

His struggle to feed his family, despite not having a lot of money, and while at the same time earnestly striving to think and do what is good, will lead to the experiencing of those conditions and happenings that may appear miraculous to him. This is because such happenings as he would experience would lie beyond the boundaries of his current expectations, which (his expectations) are always very narrow when compared to the range of what is *actually* possible in accordance with the working of the Laws of Creation, as it affects the spiritual species.

He is able to experience how those things that he truly needs, spiritually and physically, come to him through pathways that he has never considered open to him, and also in ways that force him to think and act differently from how he has hitherto thought and acted. Through these experiences his conceptions of the way things work and are capable of working in the Universe, in Creation, change. This expansion in his conception is *spiritual growth,* and also impacts on the nature of his perceptive capacity in an ennobling way. His capacity to expand intuitively into different worlds of possibilities broadens the range from which he can draw spiritual currents as fruit of his perception, his *intuitive* perception.

He would see his goal and his task in Creation as involving more than just the earth and the satisfaction of his lowly physical needs, and would discover a world of possibilities for the experiencing of happiness which would be much broader than anything he could have previously imagined, because the earthbound intellect which he had relied upon until then could not think itself out of the *purely earthly* conceptions of how things work and come together.

The intellect is only able to give form to the outermost ramifications of the spiritual volition. It is needed to put into earthly form that which comes from the spirit within. As such it is only able to see or perceive the final and most superficial form of every happening, but never the beginning of the process, which lies in realms forever inaccessible to it. The beginning of the process lies at the core of the happening as seed. This seed is the intuitive feeling or perception that led to the development of the thoughts and actions that have given rise to the conditions that man has to experience in the present. That which becomes perceptible to the intellect lies on the surface; it serves only as a cloak for that which has been willed by the spirit, and which has developed and become perceptible also to the physical senses, as a channel for the experiencing of the particular volition in the physical world. It helps determine the form of the outer or physical condition through which the fruit of intuitive feeling returns to the producer for his tasting or experiencing of it. The activity of the intellect is in the outermost realm of every happening and every manifestation, and it is only this aspect of the happenings that it is able to see and examine.

Being a product of the physical brain, the intellect is limited to the attractive capacity that corresponds to what is earthly. It lacks the motivating power that is borne by the spirit, and can only interact with the final ramifications of spiritual movement. This movement, which is brought about by the attractive nature of the spirit, as it makes use of and transmits the neutral Power resting in Creation, is what we refer to as life. It is however only the consequence of Life proper, Which is God. It is the movement that results from the effects of the Radiation of Life. Only the spirit is able to make direct contact with a form of this Radiation, and it passes it on as it vibrates in accordance with its own nature. This passing on must take place prior to any of the effects reaching the brain, which then forms the intellect.

The intellect, being a product of something of the same substance as the earth (the frontal brain), and correspondingly limited in its movement and its attractive capacity, is bound to a certain degree of perception and can never exceed this. There is only so much that it can pull together in its attempt at forming an understanding. It cannot interact with anything *unearthly* in this attempt. A sharp limitation is placed on it by virtue of its origin. Thus it cannot make sense of what is beneficial to the human spirit, whose origin lies in a much higher plane, with a correspondingly higher frequency of vibration, and with the capacity to follow the process from spiritual volition (seed) to earthly condition (final ramification of fruit). Intellectual work without spiritual backing is therefore just as useful as an empty shell, without any support, and bound to implode or collapse just when it is supposed to yield fruit.

When man makes his volition primarily the desiring for what is earthly, he also directs the energy meant for the animation of the spirit mainly towards the intellect, which, through being one-sidedly used as a result, becomes over-exerted and over-cultivated, at the expense of spiritual movement and expansion or growth. This one-sided development of the intellect leads to or occurs simultaneously with one's development of increased spiritual sluggishness and indolence, and an increase in one's inability to *see* beyond the earthly side of things; an inability to see what lies at the heart or core of the happenings around him and the conditions that he has to live through.

The associated lack of spiritual movement would mean a contracting of the spirit, a reduction in the attractive capacity of the human spirit concerned, and a corresponding reduction in the flow of spiritual currents from above through the spirit (contracted) in question.

The spiritual current from above is the energy needed for growth and *development* in Creation. It is the creative energy needed for growth and expansion. So, a reduction in the amount of spiritual currents from above, from the Light, also makes itself felt in the physical surroundings of man on earth, in the availability or lack thereof of resources of various kinds. The undeveloped or starved spirit is less able to pull together through attraction that which it would need from the material world around it. It cannot get away from the feeling of being in need, even when it may have access to a lot of money and other physical resources. It cannot recognise the true nature of what it has around it and how to apply it rightly. It cannot bring it to that state of readiness for use. It cannot form it in the right way through the process and steps already described above. It is wasteful.

The resulting one-sidedness envelops the spirit like a cloak or a veil, because it develops and forms itself around the spirit like everything else the spirit feels. It is a particular kind of vibration with corresponding homogeneous effects. Its weight pulls the affected spirit down to a corresponding plane. It takes on form just like the envy energy-form does, and also manifests on earth in corresponding forms or conditions, bringing to man and causing him to see and recognise only that which agrees with the one-sidedness that he bears within. What flows from his *pure* spiritual core to his earthly surroundings, and what goes in towards this core from outside of the physical cloak, is forced to pass though this envelop or cloak of one-sidedness (formed with the layers of lighter material substances), and is thus correspondingly altered or dimmed. The transmitted picture is skewed accordingly. As a result, only caricatures of what should develop take on form and grow, as evidence of how he has made use of the creative currents available to him from above.

A man with such an inclination will interpret the happenings in his surroundings according to how they agree or disagree with his one-sided and limited picture or conception of what will bring him happiness. In this regard he will only consider things from the earthly point of view. Even if he were to believe in some form of existence after physical death, he will imagine it according to this his earthly and very limited conception. It is also in this manner that he will interpret the concepts of love, help, fortune, success, and so on. His idea of how to fight and what to fight for will also be correspondingly affected. He will therefore look for definite conditions in his search for peace and happiness, and miss the help that comes to him in the moment-by-moment conditions of his earth-life.

For, in each of these moments exists the opportunity for him to recognise how he can sever and be free from the connections that he maintains to base and dark entities (such as those of envy, greed, fear, selfishness, conceit, vanity, spiritual ignorance, narrow-mindedness, and so on), and form for himself those kinds that will aid his recognition of the Will of the Light and thus the path for his spiritual ascent.

But in the course of his search for specific desired conditions, he will oppose everything that is meant to help him, because it will be different from the narrow and specific picture that he holds about the way things work and how he has to act to get what he feels he needs, desires or even deserves. So, not only does he miss the help that is given to him in the conditions that form for him, but he also actively obstructs the recognition of such help by the rest of mankind through what he spreads about it in his thoughts and with his actions and words.

All the warnings that come from within him as intuitive percep-tions, as his Inner Voice, are readily disregarded, with the aim of sup-pressing them. This is because he has his eye on specific earthly goals and conditions, and such warnings from within only serve to, in his view, interfere with their attainment, that is, if he at all still hears them.

This happens naturally because, with the volition of the spirit di-rected mainly towards what is earthly, most of the energy absorbed by him is directed towards the intellect, which is charged with forming the earthly environment according to the volition of the spirit. With such influx of power currents the intellect is brought to greater movement than is the spirit, causing it to become over-developed when compared to the spirit, and thus causing it to assume a superior position over the spirit as it tries to always have its way. This position of superiority is brought about simply through the overdevelopment of the overfed in-tellect and the simultaneous malnourishment of the spirit, leading to the latter's increased sluggishness and weakness.

This nature and direction of focus of the spiritual volition become for men the determining factors of how things ought to be and also how they actually develop, because the volition of the spirit is directed mainly towards earthly things. With this the spirit expresses its desire to attract to itself only that which will aid in the attainment of earthly goals. So, through this act the one concerned becomes subject to the leadership of the earthbound intellect, which cannot perceive anything beyond what is earthly. He becomes subject to the world in which the intellect has control. He is not able to get the full picture of any happening in order to respond aright and form the right kind of environment for spiritual growth and ascent, as well as for physical well-being in a paradise-like state on earth. The master (the spirit) places itself beneath the tool (the intellect).

In this way, the intellect naturally stands in the way of any spiritual awakening, because spiritual awakening would mean the non-attainment of those goals towards which the wrongly-empowered intellect naturally strives. As long as the gaze remains directed mainly towards narrow earthly desires and goals, the spirit of man languishes in a sleep towards spiritual death.

Such sleep, undisturbed, leads to complete cessation of movement, with the natural end of the breakdown of the spiritual personality formed so far, and reversion back to unconscious spirit seed.

As he develops downwards in this state of sleep he will react to happenings around him with such deep feelings, thoughts and actions as stem from envy, fear, distrust, anger, narrow-mindedness, superficiality, conceit, spiritual ignorance, and so on, which all act together because they grow out of one another due to their relatedness.

They manifest his disagreement with how things have developed, i.e., how differently they have formed from the narrow picture that he holds within. That picture which is formed through the narrowness of his intellectual perception. The energy-forms of these emotions, thoughts and actions then go on to influence what manifests on earth for him, making it even more difficult for him to see, and dragging him further downwards towards the depths of utter spiritual darkness, which is the ultimate destination of his journey along the path formed ahead of him by his volition of one-sidedness. He blinds himself to real life and to the only chance of sustained existence.

In this state of darkness, his perception is even narrower and his reaction to what has formed for him as fruit of his volition gets even worse, because in the meantime the forms of envy, fear, the struggle for earthly power and influence, conceit, and so on, have all grown and developed further due to the link that he maintains with them, and through which he supplies them with nourishing neutral power and creative spiritual currents. The link is maintained as long as he has not severed his connections with them through the right recognition, change of attitude and redirection of spiritual currents, thus, of animating energy.

Through the same link, he also receives, in the reciprocal effect of the happening, reinforcing feedback of base currents for his thoughts and his volition, from those realms to which the base forms belong, making it difficult for him to see differently and to change his attitude, because his works form around him and hold him down to their weight and perceptive level. Each of the energy-forms that he produces with the power to attract sends its own specific effects into the loom of Creation, which weaves for him the carpet of his fate. The final form, which he experiences as a condition on earth, is therefore a combination of the effects of several intuitive and thought forms, developed by him in response to several impressions from his surroundings in his past.

★   ★   ★

In the manifestation on earth of these conditions, as has been mentioned already, even the combinations between the smallest atomic substances are affected accordingly, because their individual vibrations correspond and adapt to the effects of the more powerful forms produced by men with spiritual power; that power with which they are supposed to develop the earth through upward-striving activity. These combinations produce diseased forms if the nature of the vibration of the spiritual around them is weak and slow. From these basic levels or building blocks the earthly surroundings of man were formed, according to the strongest and prevailing spiritual volition.

Mankind on earth, over several millennia, drew steadily away from the Light and the perception of the guidance from It, and strove more towards the desiring for earthly pleasures and earthly power and influence. With their thoughts they steadily nourished those forms that made it increasingly more difficult for them to know the Will of the Light, the Will of God, or to even *want to know* this Will. Their surroundings formed and developed accordingly. In them manifested the base forms that men expressed in their thoughts, with their words and actions.

The desire to even know this Will waned increasingly as man developed and nourished the notion that it must be difficult, if not impossible, to know and abide by It. Increasingly men grew to believe that they stood to lose something, some earthly ground to others seeking similar earthly goals, if they devoted attention and effort towards this most worthy of causes. As a result they never really came to know of the true benefits of abiding by this Will. They never came to know this Will. It never became an earnest desire within men, one which surpassed everything in its importance.

So, the vegetation and landscape formed and changed accordingly over time, including the deserts, water bodies, the air, the layers of the atmosphere, the make-up of the earth underground, the development of the bodies, the manner of living and habitats of animals, the changes and developments of the bodies of men, beginning at the most basic level (DNA), the nature of craftsmanship, music, government and leadership, arts, entertainment, movies, everything, all adjusted to the nature of the prevailing volition among men, which was a dark and low one. They formed in such ways as would give to man what he expressed the desire to experience through the way in which he formed his inner life.

This inevitably also affected the nature of the institutions formed by men to deal with education, healthcare, money management, marketing systems, and so on. These institutions developed as one-sidedly as mankind did, with regard only for what led to an increase in earthly power and influence, thus for the purely physical and superficial, without concern as to their effects on the development of the spiritual and animating core of man. They all took corresponding shape along with developing mankind in their varied races, cultures, groups and nations.

In the course of this development, particular groups or nations of men rose to certain heights at particular periods in time, but due to the fact that they were formed wrongly, they could not advance further since they could not bring up the necessary vibration to cross the necessary threshold for this. The emptiness and shakiness of the foundations upon which they had built, which were largely based on calculations of the lifeless and earthbound intellect, revealed themselves as the fruits of the pursuits of men. Each of these nations in turn fell back down low as a people on earth, or even, in some cases, completely disappeared in a kind of extinction or disintegration, after having reached particular influential heights.

Had they maintained the right movement within, they would have been able to go through the storms that came at certain periods in time, which were Cosmic Turning-Points, and advanced as new people into the new times, which marked further stages in the development of all mankind, the earth and the material world.

The same happening repeated itself time and again, with peoples of various kinds rising to great heights only to fall into near or complete oblivion afterwards. At such critical periods or points in time, mankind also received opportunities for advancements in their knowledge of Creation, so that they could develop upward. Similar to the way in which a plant goes through the various stages of its development from seed to germination, growth, flowering and fruiting, while receiving everything that it needs for each stage of this development when it needs it.

Such times also came with upheavals and so-called natural disasters, because changes had to be made also to the topography of the earth to accommodate the vibrations and forms of the new time. Great numbers of men lost their lives at such times and severe shocks of various kinds reverberated through the souls of men, causing them to temporarily let go of their attachments to their material interests and allow for the penetration of light rays through new teachings brought to them about Creation. But had men been developing in the right way the changes at such critical times would have only brought joy to them, clear signs of progress upwards and a graduation to a higher state of perception and recognition.

In the early beginnings these teachings were brought by spiritual beings from planes higher than the origin of the spirit-germs that came to matter and to earth to develop and mature (the spirit of man). These higher spiritual beings came to help the developing spiritual beings (men) on earth towards the next higher step in their grasping of the Will of God, Which manifests as the easily recognizable Laws of Nature or Laws of Creation.

With a better grasping of these happenings the developing human spirits could direct their volition more towards what leads to the Light, since this is indispensible for the drawing of currents from the Light in the reciprocal effect of such a focus. What they drew down from the Heights would help them mature, as well as flow to their material surroundings in an upbuilding manner. The periodic changes in the forms that developed in matter, due to changes in the vibrations of the cloaked spirit particles in matter, were supposed to correspond with an elevation in the state of luminosity and beauty in the World of Matter. They came at times when the earth was to be elevated to a higher state or orbit. This would have coincided with the attainment of a higher state of maturity within the human spirits developing on earth.

As already mentioned, these stages of development are similar to what one would find in any material cycle of development, which always goes through the process of sowing, development and maturation, flowering and bearing of fruit, and then disintegration to the basic units for the purpose of reformation in a newer, nobler form. This is an eternally repeating process that takes place only in the material planes of Creation, because the material world itself is a cloak for developing spiritual and animistic substances and, as such, cannot maintain a permanent form. In the course of a normal development, the forming each time of nobler forms leads to the absorption of energy and the increased animation of the basic particles involved in the forming, which then go on to combine again into new forms following a process of disintegration of the old forms.

The human spirit developing in matter also partakes of this development, since it is in matter and is connected to it through the various material cloaks that it bears around it. At the different Turning-Points, energy (spiritual currents) is able to flow more freely to certain human spirits open to it, aided by the upheavals, the so-called natural disasters and shocking experiences, which often come during these transformational periods, and which help loosen man's attachment to mainly earthly concerns. As a part of their effects these happenings give to man the fruits of his past deeds and help him see himself as he really stands, thereby providing him with the impetus and opportunity to change his inner attitude for the attraction of a brighter and more conscious state in his future.

Help came through those specially prepared for the task at such points in the past. Following the spiritual beings from higher planes or origins than earthmen's, at subsequent Cosmic Turning-Points, came the prophets who were blessed with the ability to see better than other men the connections necessary for man to recognize the workings of the Laws of Creation.

The prophets came to help men see better the workings that brought them their fate, so that in acting accordingly they would come to personally experience the nature of the Will of God, Which shows Itself in the Laws of Creation, which are the same as the Laws of Nature. A change in their attitude in this regard would have led to the development of more harmonious and peaceful ethereal and physical environments, in which everything that developed would have had a beneficial effect on the development of the spiritual personalities concerned.

The help brought to mankind at those points in time, however, were mostly met with hostility from men, whose spiritual indolence and wish to hang on to the comfortable old had so developed that they had a paralyzing effect on men's capacity to move inwardly, i.e., spiritually. As a result they could not wake up and could not recognize and make use of the help brought. They could not bring up from within them the desire for it. On the particular paths that they were on they had no desire for what was brought to them.

Those who cared to listen soon turned the teachings into religions with rigid doctrines, without grasping aright their true import, and also without truly applying them to life on earth, as well as in the world of their thoughts and that of their deep inner feelings or perceptions, in order to gain spiritually from them. Only the right understanding and application of the teachings could have led to the growth of the human spirit from one stage of awareness to the next. For, the next step of development could not be attained until the necessary previous one had been properly and fully grasped.

Without the necessary inward change brought about through inner, spiritual exertion, mankind continued to sink lower and deeper. Their situation grew even worse because then they assumed that they had received a pass to enlightenment because they belonged to some religion or other. They became more spiritually languid as a consequence of this false conception, which led them to think that they had what they needed and did not need anything more. The reduced intensity of vibration associated with this lack of inner movement and desiring for what comes from the Light above, closed them off to all that could move them to truly seek the path to the Light.

Their spiritual rigidity grew, being subject to the Law of Development in matter, making it even more difficult for new and necessary knowledge to penetrate to them. They remained destined for destruction through disintegration, together with the material world at the time when the latter would have to fall apart in order to form itself anew. The falling-apart would include the tearing of the spirit of man from the spiritual conceptions that he has wrongly formed here in matter, and which have taken on base or dark forms that are in need of disassembly and destruction. Through its connection to these wrong conceptions, the spirit of man connects itself to that which must undergo disintegration and a grinding to primordial dust (seed). This process is then experienced by the spirit in the torturous state that has been termed spiritual death or damnation.

This is the fate of those who bind themselves to matter through their desiring mainly for earthly pleasures and gain, and who, as a result of this binding, do not steadily mature and ascend out of matter before it gets to the point of *transformation through disintegration* in the course of its ongoing cycle of development.

This disintegration must take place one celestial globe at a time and one part of matter at a time. Every human spirit on earth has to be wary of this potential trap.

The suffering among men continued to increase and change in form, because the superficial remedies that men sought to implement towards them did not change their inner natures or attitudes, which constituted the starting points of the problems that became expressed in their earthly conditions. The darkness had so spread on earth and its ethereal surroundings that men could no longer see their way out of their entanglements on their own. They cried out for help in various ways.

The Light began to prepare help for mankind, destined for the present time, in time for a Final Turning-Point; a time when a final separation would have to be made between what serves the Light in an upbuilding manner and what stands as a hindrance, obstructing this process. A time when the spirits of men should already be separating from matter, as they make their final departure from its planes and ascend upwards to their origin in the completion of the cycle of their development to full consciousness. When matter itself must undergo the necessary process of disintegration in order to form itself anew as fertile soil for the future cloaking and harbouring of new energy-forms, which will be in need of further development and maturation.

Prophesies made their way through open human spirits to mankind of the coming of a strong Helper, Who would battle the Darkness and link the willing back with the Light. The prophesies were interpreted by men from different cultures and were also interpreted differently, but they all mostly led to the expectation of a Helper from the Light.

As men sank deeper, however, it became evident that there would not be any anchorage for the Light at the appointed time for the dissemination of the intended help. Mankind would have been too far gone to be able to take in and make use of this help. There would not even have been any opening for an entrance by One from the Light in a world so darkened as would have been the case had everything continued the way it was developing.

Some, however, who did not deserve to go to disintegration with decaying matter, would have been left without any help if this were allowed to happen. These were ones who still had a spark of longing for the Light, which had not yet been completely extinguished through the influence of the burgeoning darkness, expressed through the majority of mankind.

For the sake of these few, the Light intervened.

The humanly inconceivable Love of the Light would come into this dark world, in spite of the potential for the worst kinds of hostilities which It might face, since It was coming into alien territory, a part of Creation which already belonged to the Realm of Darkness because of how wrongly the available power currents had been used. The perfect Justice of God, Which always works with Divine Love, made this happening inevitable, for those who had to be helped because they sowed the seeds for it could not be left without the necessary help. For the sake of the few that fell into this category at that time, Jesus incarnated, in the most natural way, into a physical body specially prepared for Him. A Spark of Divine Energy thereby made entry onto the earth-plane.

His task was to show those willing to listen how they should act in order to realign their spiritual resolve or desiring upwards towards the Light, in the midst of the darkness that surrounded them as their *own* work. To do this He walked the earth outwardly a man but inwardly a Part of Primordial Light. He confronted the temptations that plagued men and the base radiations that streamed at them with the purity of His intuitive perception. The intuitive perception is the lever used by man to direct neutral creative power, through the forming and expression of his innermost desires, for the development of his world and his fate. It originates within man and sends out specific kinds of radiations or vibrations, good or evil, to its surroundings.

The base vibrations present on earth and its ethereal surroundings had to fall back from Jesus through a process of repulsion due to a lack of homogeneity. There was therefore no basis for an attraction and the necessary contact needed for influencing. Through His Being and what emanated from Him, He was able to create an opening through the surrounding and enveloping darkness for those who wished to ascend to the Heights of Light. Through His Nature He paved a path for those who sought a way upwards through the canopy of darkness which had formed above men, blocking their spiritual view and preventing their spiritual ascent and maturation.

This canopy of darkness felt to men as that which kept them from even desiring or wanting to know what would benefit them spiritually, as well as lead to more ennobled and joyous earthly surroundings.

Only One so strong could cleave a path through this canopy of Darkness to the Light, so that men's thoughts and volitions could once more go upwards, the only way that they could draw down the needed spiritual currents (energy) in the reciprocal effect of their *own* upward-tending volitions, their thoughts and actions. The reciprocal effects of their upward-tending volitions were to enlighten them and encourage them along a path that would lead to the formation of those works and environments which would help them ascend. Those who could take advantage of this could then keep the spark alight within them and develop it to a flame, in order later on to be able to recognize what help would be sent to earth in the time of the Final Turning-Point, which was then approaching.

However, outside of a few simple-minded individuals, who truly wished to adopt the principles that Jesus brought, many found it difficult to leave their old, wrong and deep-seated habits and ways of thinking. Some of these were people who considered themselves to be well-versed in the Laws and so did not need anything new. Others, who were higher up in the leadership of the religious community, feared that the new teaching would disrupt the influence that they had at the time on their flock, which gave them positions of earthly power and authority; therefore they worked against Jesus for that reason.

Some of the members of the religious community, who were expecting the Messiah, had expectations of what the Messiah was to do, how He was to do it, the conditions (as they interpreted the prophesies) that had first to be present on the ground prior to His arrival on earth, and the automatic consequences that were to result from His presence on earth.

One amongst many of the expectations of the people at the time involved the immediate physical deliverance of the Jews at the time from the oppressive conditions in which they lived under the rule of the Romans.

In fact, each person at that time who had given some thought to the matter, and who considered himself a believer, also held a picture of how he perceived the coming of the expected Messiah. This picture was unique to the inner nature of the one concerned, and differed from *every other one*. The absence of the true and personal striving for the Truth prevented them from recognising that which accorded with the Truth, and which had to be a common thread that ran through every picture that arose from a pure striving to know the Will of God.

The striving to know and abide by the Laws of Creation, as human beings and not as mere animals, with corresponding capacities and responsibilities, would have led them to recognition of the Truth, even if the individual paths to this took on different forms. This is because the Truth would have provided them individually with the answers to the inevitable questions that would have confronted them along such upward-tending paths. Only one who was truly awake in this would have appreciated what was brought. Recognition of the Truth could not have been kept from him by any force.

It needs not be specially mentioned here that none of such expectations as men had then, which were largely based on very narrow and earthly interpretations of the prophesies that spoke of the Coming of a Messiah, came close to reflecting the actual Mission of the Messiah. A right understanding of this Mission would have also at the same time brought about the right attitude within the expectant one, and also the right degree of humility and openness to help from the Light, in light of how deeply man had fallen. Only such humility and the associated openness could have allowed him to recognize and voluntarily adapt to the newly-brought extension to the then existing knowledge of the governing Laws of God.

But men mostly had expectations of the fulfillments of personal desires and wishes, which were mostly earthly in nature. The idea that the *actual* Will of God be first sought and carried out by them, as the starting point of all fulfillments, was very distant from their mode of thinking.

So, Jesus had to first meet the criteria that *they* had set for the Messiah before they could accept *Him* as such.

There were many reasons why men did not receive the help brought to them, which required great effort and a great deal of preparation that took thousands of years to develop. But always it was the dark attributes adopted and developed by men that kept them from recognizing Jesus and the help that He brought mankind. The rigid conceptions that men held within them kept them from recognizing things as they really were, and not just as they thought they should be.

Had men been working to rid themselves of base attitudes and attributes, such as spiritual indolence, the craving for earthly power and influence, greed, narrow-mindedness (which, in addition to many other things, served to keep men's gaze focused mainly or solely on earthly benefits), conceit, distrust, fear, anxiety, etc., they would have recognized more readily *that* which bore truth. This is so because in the course of battling their own faults they would have come to see glimpses of the real nature of the Truth. They would have been able to recognise true courage and strength, such as would have been evident in the actions of the Bringer of Truth.

Those who did receive some of what Jesus brought became encouraged to hope and to look upwards in their volition, towards the

Heights of the Light, especially after Jesus had died on the cross whilst still maintaining His position regarding the Truth and His High Mission. His lack of wavering even in the face of certain death touched many and caused them to see the authenticity in His assertions and His words. A wavering in this regard would have caused many to regard Him as just one of the many claimants of Divinity at the time, and their already well-developed distrust would have led them to forget everything that Jesus had brought and taught. But they could feel the conviction behind His words, and the energy inherent in this conviction, which was not to be found any place else on earth, made a strong impression upon those open to it; for all energy-forms have specific and corresponding kinds of effects.

What people were able to perceive through the nature of Jesus encouraged them to keep hope alive, and not to allow the resolve within them for what is good to die in the face of all the darkness that they were surrounded by, which ruled on earth at the time. This resolve is necessary for the right development of all human spirits, because what forms for man remains the fruit of what he sows with his inner attitude (his inner resolve), his thoughts, words and actions. This basic fact cannot be changed regarding the nature of the working-out of the abilities of the spirit.

The great sacrifice made, therefore, by Jesus, the Son of God, was His coming to this dark and antagonistic-to-the-Light part of Creation, in order to show men how they could perceive the happenings around them in the right manner, so that in their reactions to these happenings they would not produce forms (works) that would further entangle them and cause them to sink even deeper, as the reciprocal effects of these works returned to them for reaping. He came to show men how to make the right use of the energy coursing through Creation for up-building works of all kinds. He came to show them how to be good transmitters of energy for their own salvation from darkness and resurrection from matter.

In other words, He came to help men recognise the working of the Laws of Creation, and thereby experience and know the proper mode of transmission of this energy; to recognize the Divine Justice and strict logic that lie in every happening. But He could do nothing where a particular human spirit had resolved not to hear His words and to continue along his old path, because the free will of man to decide his fate cannot be taken away from him. It is a part of the natural working of his spiritual abilities which cannot be changed, for, as he calls it so does it form for him.

Neither could Jesus take upon Himself the guilt incurred by those people who, through their own acts of will, drew to themselves particular kinds of energy-forms and radiations as reciprocal effects. He could take upon himself the guilt of no one. According to the Law of Sowing and Reaping, this is an impossible act. It cannot happen, because it is not possible for it to happen. In a complete cycle, that which emanates from one always returns to him. It may not have as heavy an impact as it might have had in its original form only if the person has, in the course of the development to maturation of that which has issued from him, changed his attitude to something better and lighter at the time of the returning impact. But come back to him it must, in one form or another.

The cycle once opened must come to a close in order to cease to exist as a functioning unit, in order for the action to be redeemed. That which comes back to one on earth in the form of a condition or a happening is redemption for that which he put into form on earth. The ethereal form placed in a corresponding ethereal sphere of matter, forming the basis for man's thinking and his physically visible actions, continues to live on as long as the person concerned still maintains the kind of inner attitude that brought it together as a living form in the first place. Only when he has changed in this regard, that is, only when his inner nature has become sufficiently different due to a different way of viewing the issue, can he cease supplying the developed ethereal form with corresponding strengthening currents. Only then could the form wither away, cease to exist and stop having a corresponding influence on him.

In the meantime, however, it will continue to contribute to what forms the inner nature of the one concerned, as well as to the development of similar forms produced by others. The outer, final effects of this nature will continue to manifest in his earthly or physically visible actions, leading to his needing to continually atone for the seeds sown with such actions if they oppose the Laws of Nature.

So, the closure of the cycle of development of a particular action carried out by a man on earth, which comes with the reaping of the reciprocal effect of it, is redemption as well as atonement only for that particular earthly action, but not also for the forms produced through his thinking, which remain bound to him, and which, in the first place, formed the basis for the particular action. It could still remain in existence in spite of the fact that one of the cycles opened on earth as a result of an action based on this inner nature has come to its own end. The existing intuitive or thought-form that led to the physical action atoned for, could still continue to influence the forming of other physical deeds which, in the closing of their cycles, continue to demand from their originator atonement and redemption.

So, he could go on for a long time opening up cycles that need to close or be redeemed through painful experiences, as long as he does not change the basis for such earthly actions (his inner attitude) and thus change the earthly actions.

If the reciprocal effect of the action, which is really a gross material manifestation of his inner attitude, also induces him to change inwardly, then he could bring to a close the cycle of development of the particular ethereal or thought-form that made possible the manifestation of the initial outward action. So, a person who physically reacts angrily or fearfully does so because of the existing fear or anger forms ethereally connected to him, which took on their particular forms when the one concerned inwardly felt fearful or angry on a previous occasion, and which he continued to nourish by maintaining the basis for the fearful thinking - a particular kind of inner attitude.

If he does not change his attitude with regards to these feelings he will continue to nourish the forms of his fear and anger, so that they grow and develop and continue to influence his physical actions, and thus manifest themselves in the physical deed.

The experiencing of the effect of the ethereal form, for example, the form of fear or envy, is the reciprocal or return-effect of the initial act of producing this form. The experiencing of the reciprocal effect provides the one concerned with the opportunity to cease the nourishment of the form, and thus bring its cycle of development to a close. It allows him to taste of it and experience its effect, so that he can voluntarily decide to stop contributing to its existence through his nourishing of said emotions.

The experiencing of the effects of the fear or envy, for example, and the adequate inner change in attitude as a result of such an experience, are atonement and redemption from being bound to the ethereal and physical forms and their effects, and also forgiveness for the one who placed them in Creation through his intuitive perceiving, thinking, speaking and acting. He is forgiven when he has made right what he caused to develop wrongly. This also includes *all* the effects that his actions might have had on the spiritual and physical conditions of others.

While the physical returning effect brings to a close the cycle of a particular physical action, his inner attitude and way of *perceiving* or seeing must change in order for him to become separated from the corresponding and preceding ethereal form. This is because the particular ethereal form is linked to him through a particular kind of spiritual decision, a spiritual volition or attitude. A change in this attitude leads to the formation of something different, which corresponds to the new attitude, and the starvation of the old form, which no longer receives nourishment for its sustenance and can then wither away.

If in the meantime his works have had a negative impact on the development of another, then he must remain bound to that other person through the link thus created until the harm done has been made right, no matter how long this process takes. If the reciprocal action for an earthly act does not come in one lifetime, then it may come in another, for it is the spirit of the one concerned that is bound and not the physical body.

The only way that a person could learn of the actual nature of his actions is by directly tasting of their fruits. Anything other than this would leave room for spiritual ignorance and for the certainty of a repetition of the wrong action in his thinking, his speaking or his physically visible deeds. This would naturally not help the one concerned, nor would it help Creation as a whole. For, at a later date, this person would express just that which he had always held within him, but which he had not tried to change because he had no reason to think of it as wrong or harmful, or, as happens in many cases, because he did not realize that he still harboured dark volitions within him. Without the pressure to do so he would simply see no reason why he should bother himself to do so.

It is impossible for anyone to take from another what is spiritually due to return to him as the fruit of the seed he sowed in the process of exercising his free will. As Jesus already taught men, "whatever a man sows, that shall he reap, many times over". This can be seen in any process of development, and clearly presents itself in the farm field where a seed of a particular kind yields many more corresponding fruits and seeds than the actual number of seeds sown.

Through this process man is also supposed to decide whether or not he wishes to participate in the upbuilding that must happen now in the setting up of a Kingdom of Peace here on earth; a Kingdom of God. He must decide whether or not he wishes to be a part of this Kingdom, and return fully conscious to the Spiritual Realm whence he left as an unconscious seed-germ in the beginning of the cycle of his development to self-consciousness. There, upon his re-entry, he would have developed into a useful fruit that is able to serve in Creation as it should; a fully developed transmitter of energy. One that transmits without dimming what comes from above, and which thus participates in the expansion of Creation.

It is the spiritual indolence, the love of comfort and ease, the ignorance and conceit of men, that allow many to believe that it could be possible for the Light to send a Part of Itself down to the lowly realms of the darkened earth, so that It could take the burden off of the shoulders of little, ungrateful and conceited earthmen, and place this burden upon Itself, just so that those who incurred the debts, and who were well-equipped by their Maker to settle them, would avoid dealing with them! It is a kind of thinking that can only come from a mankind that has sunken so far from the Light that it can no longer detect the gross lack of logic and the absurdity in such a manner of reasoning! He cannot see how defiling this notion is of the purity and perfection of the Justice of God!

The assertion that the Love of God is unimaginably great and cannot be fully understood by man is a true one, but it does not excuse man's ignorance of the true nature of the perceptible expressions of this Love, and of the happenings within those planes from which he is well-equipped, as a human spirit, to intuitively perceive. The capacity to intuitively perceive was given to him for the purpose of understanding the Will of his Creator, and for transmitting this understanding through his being into the various planes that he is connected to; the earth being the coarsest of such planes along the normal course that he has to travel for his development.

Only through the right understanding could he have any hopes of living in accordance with this Will, and only the species that is able to adjust to the working of this Will can maintain itself in Creation, which itself is governed and kept fresh by this same working. Everything else is ground to dust as soon as it has proved itself to be useless in the necessary upbuilding in Creation.

Divine Love came to show man how to recognise this working so that he could free himself from base energy-forms and produce those kinds of forms and vibrations that could help him upwards. In this lie his salvation and his liberation from darkness, his redemption and his resurrection from the material world into his spiritual origin, the Paradise of the human spirits developing in matter.

A lack of understanding of this process cannot prevent the natural consequence of it, because it is solely the nature of the radiation which man emanates that determines what forms for him and what he attracts to himself. It is in this working that the Perfection of the Light shows itself to him; he sees the perfect working of Divine Justice in the agreement between *cause* and *effect*, sowing and reaping. But because he often thinks too much of himself, he assumes that God will watch over him personally, and that He will not allow any harm to befall him as long as he continues to maintain only outwardly and with empty words that he believes in Him and in His Son, Jesus.

Again, this thinking only fosters weaknesses such as I have already given examples of. These weaknesses are wrongly formed and developed conceptions, which came into being through the indolence of the human spirits developing on earth and in other planes in the World of Matter. At the same time as this spiritual indolence was developing, the over-cultivation of and over-reliance upon the intellect of the frontal brain was growing on earth. One could not happen without the other, because the indestructible energy that was supposed to flow towards the development of the spirit was diverted towards the one-sided growth of the intellect – which remains bound to a limited range of perception.

The frontal brain and its product, the intellect, became one-sidedly over-developed as a result of the unbalanced direction of energy currents to them, causing man to sow death and destruction already at the foundation of his thoughts, words and actions, which all bore one-sidedness and lack of balance within them. The works and conceptions formed in this manner, that is, whilst relying on the perception of the intellect, could not include the perception of the spirit, which is not bound to the limitations of the earth-bound intellect, and thus is able to transmit what is beneficial to the human being.

They were bound to lead to destruction, no matter how nicely formed they appeared. From the very beginning such works did not harbor life within them because they were devoid of spirit, which is the energy that brings about movement in Creation; that movement which gives the semblance of life, which transmits the radiation of Life-proper through Creation. All else is empty and will collapse upon itself when it has to show its fruit at the time of its harvest.

This was the result of the tasting of the wrong fruit, the fruit of the one-sided focus on earthly matters by mankind; the *original sin*, which led downwards to all the other developments along a false and detrimental path. I have already described this development, but it is important to see the role that this diversion of power played in man's misuse of the help that was sent to him on several occasions by the Light.

★　★　★

After the brief stay on earth of the Son of God (which means "a Part of God") Jesus Christ, it became possible once again for the thoughts of men to rise upwards in the direction of the Divine Heights. Without this intervention, it would have become impossible centuries later for mankind still to seriously contemplate issues concerning God and the reason for their being, and to inwardly have a true yearning for something from such Heights as where the life-sustaining Power comes into Creation.

The superficiality and moral decadence that would have been very deeply ingrained in the psyche of men at that time would have developed further and swept over mankind even more completely, so that there would not have been any chance for the sprouting of anything light, which alone could bring about the attraction from above of corresponding energy currents to fuel the growth of this light seedling. The coming and presence on earth of Jesus greatly slowed down the decaying process for many, and made possible a future anchorage of Help through another Envoy from the Light, as He, Jesus, had promised would happen.

But mankind in general continued to sink into the realms of darkness, because a great majority of so-called believers did not apply in their lives the teachings that He brought, and so did not truly change the nature of the vibrations within them. They did not recognise through personal experience the reason to base their every inner and outer movement on the new knowledge that they had been given, for they did not strive to truly understand what had been given. They regarded everything too superficially, too much in the earthly sense to which they had become bound, thus, through the veils or lenses that had formed around them through this one-sided way of seeing and thinking.

Many, therefore, continued to harbour desires and wishes that were primarily earthly in nature, and so they did not bring themselves to greater spiritual movement and consciousness. They did not seek out the spiritual implications of the happenings around them, but only re-acted to them according to the nature of the earthly wishes and desires that they still harboured deep within them. Their interactions with their fellow-men not only revealed their true inner natures, but also left the wrong impressions on the latter about the true nature of the *worship* of God.

The greater portion of those who regarded themselves as believers gave up the right to investigate for themselves what the Will of God really is, and submitted to being led by the narrow opinions developed within their religious groups. Since it was necessary to subscribe to such doctrines as developed from these narrow opinions in order for one to be called a member of a particular religion, it naturally followed that the believers became one-sided in their perceiving and fostered even more one-sidedness just in the process of maintaining their memberships in particular religious groups.

The necessary broadmindedness, which would have been required to grasp what came from the Light and what would benefit all of man-kind, could only have come when everyone was striving towards seeing for himself the manifestations of the Will of God in the happenings around him. He would have had to see it along *his own* path of expe-riencing, in a manner that made sense to him and left *him* convinced – convinced of a natural order and a Law that governs everything. He would have seen how this *governing* works and would have come to know and trust in its perfection, its unchanging nature. There would not have developed the confusion, fear and anxiety that are the causes of many a problem on earth today.

A great portion of those who called themselves believers not only failed to receive what was sent by God but, in fact, through their actions and their inner attitudes, actually stood between men and the true knowledge of the Will of God.

We come now to this time when people superficially go through the various rituals of their various religions on particular days of the week, while retaining and acting out in their own ways, consciously or not-so-consciously, through their thoughts, words and actions, those base attitudes that continue to develop and manifest as oppressive, difficult and dark conditions here on earth.

The activity of men, that is, the way in which they make use of the spiritual currents flowing through Creation, can be likened to what happens within a cell in the human body. The wrong use and direction by man of the energy that he has access to can be likened to what happens when a virus invades a cell in our bodies.

The virus needs the protein-production machinery of the cell in order to manufacture or produce proteins that are vital for its own development and replication. A successful invasion of a cell in the human body therefore involves the taking over of this machinery, which under normal circumstances would produce proteins such as are needed in the cells for the accurate replication, transcription and translation of human genetic material (e.g. DNA), and for the body to produce enzymes needed for a variety of functions such as the regulation of body temperature, the signaling of the onset of food digestion in the body, the production of immune cells, and so on.

After such a take-over the same machinery begins to reproduce viral proteins that are necessary for the growth and replication of viral particles (viruses) within the cell, which at this point now serves as an incubator for the invading viruses and their progeny.

When enough replication has gone on within the infected cell, the progeny, or several copies of the infecting viral particle (virus), make their way out of the used-up and now dead cell, to go and individually infect other healthy cells in the same manner. If unchecked, therefore, the viruses are able to exponentially increase in number in a relatively short period of time, while at the same time bringing about the destruction of many previously healthy cells in the human body.

The goal for the virus is to develop and multiply by any means that it is able to employ. The result for the cell of a human body is death whenever a viral particle has been able to take over its protein-production machinery, because from then on only or mainly the proteins necessary for the survival of the virus will be produced by that particular cell. The cell is either killed because of this fact or because it is tagged for destruction by certain cells of the immune system of the human body, and then possibly engulfed or destroyed by another species of immune cells.

The infected cells display some of the viral proteins produced within them on their surfaces, so that they become marked as infected cells, and are visible as such to the appropriate cells of the immune system of the human body.

The destruction of the infected cell is done for the sake of the rest of the human body, which will only survive if the destructive virus is kept from multiplying and causing more premature cell-death and tissue destruction. The successful eradication of the virus from the body therefore involves, in addition to other processes, the destruction and elimination of the infected cells.

The cells are healthy if the information or code held in the genetic material being replicated by the machinery in the cell is one that serves to promote the growth and right development of the cell. This also means that the genetic code in question must then also lead to the right and beneficial development of the human body as a whole. If the wrong code or information is inputted into the protein-production machinery of the cell, it would not develop rightly because it would lack the necessary proteins which would be necessary for various functions critical for right cell-growth and development.

When the cells of the body do not develop well the tissues of the body cannot form rightly, and this would consequently negatively affect the formation of the organs of the body. The organs of the body cannot perform optimally if they are not in good form and this would lead to premature death of the body even with the best of medical interventions.

The situation with the cell of the human body is a reflection of what happens within the human being that is earth-man. What comes from deep within him determines how his outward conditions form or develop. The outward conditions are a reflection of what he holds within, i.e., what he allows to flow through him.

The spirit of man, which has the capacity to attract, has a magnetic-pulling effect on the various species of matter. It decides what it attracts or how it brings material substances together based on how it *feels*; therefore, upon the nature of the *inner life* of man. This feeling of the spirit of man is different from the feeling that is dependent on and associated with his thinking or his thoughts. It is the intuitive perception, which gives expression to man's inner vibration. It is also the channel through which the spiritual currents from above come to him or are perceived by him. How he attunes himself within, therefore, determines what he is able to draw from above.

He draws from above using the same magnetic working of the attractive capacity of the spirit as pulls to him his earthly conditions. His volition, which is the same as his inner attitude, forms the basis for the kind of radiation that he attracts to himself. It forms the petition that he sends out into Creation as an expression of his *innermost* desire. It therefore forms the first decision that man makes in any matter. It determines the nature of everything else that develops subsequently through his thoughts, words and visible actions. As has already been mentioned earlier, it is the foundation for his thoughts.

The purer the currents that come to man through this process of attraction, the better the material world around him forms. To attract pure currents the human being concerned has therefore to maintain a corresponding inner purity. This shows itself first in his innermost attitude and desires and later also finds expression in some outward form.

The spiritual volition or direction of focus determines how the atomic and subatomic particles that develop into the forms that we are able to see and feel come together and interact for the sake of this development. So none of those changes that we often refer to as random or accidental are truly so, at least not in the way that we have mostly conceived of them. Every small and apparently insignificant stirring, every slight change in direction, shape, colour or rate of movement, everything that can be detected with the current and yet-to-be developed and produced earthly instruments, is only the after-effect of a corresponding movement within the spiritual volition of man.

These changes and movements in the physical world are always occurring in order to accommodate the prevailing volition of men, pressed out by the pressure of the power of the Light, whether good or evil, and they continue to develop through coming together in combinations until they form detectable conditions in man's environment.

These conditions form in just those ways as allow for those vibrations petitioned for by man, through the nature of his inner attunement, to come to him. He experiences the formed conditions strictly in accordance with what he allowed to emanate from him in his past, and how he stands inwardly in the present. They help him experience the fruit of what he has sown. It is in this way that he *always* reaps what he sows.

With this attractive capacity he is to draw down to earth pictures of the happenings that have already taken on form in the planes of experiencing above the earth (outside of the boundary of what is physically tangible and perceptible), to which the intellect is blinded due to its natural perceptive limitation. The pictures impress upon the spirit of one who is open to them as his *Inner Voice, Intuition or Pure Intuitive Perception.*

When heeded by man these pictures form the bases of his thoughts, words and actions, so that in living his life on earth he is able to form a bridge for the transmission of beauty and goodness in more ways than he is able to see at any given point in his development. Openness to these pictures, however, depends on the attunement of the one concerned. He has to truly want to know of that which exists above, which lets him know more about His Maker, Whose Will he must indeed come to know if he is to navigate through the material world in a manner that builds up rather than destroys. His mere wishing to know this Will is not enough. It must be his earnest volition, his innermost yearning, for this is what indeed has the capacity to attract the conditions that form around him. This innermost yearning is an expression of the living part of man (his spirit), which alone has the capacity to influence his surroundings, and which in fact is the real man!

As has been mentioned already, what man draws to himself in the form of his earthly conditions reflects what he bears within, his inner attitude, and is a part of what he has to rightly experience in order to ascend. His earthly condition serves as the means for the delivery of that which he has asked for by the way he has shaped his inner life, his inner attitude, even if at first he does not recognise that which has come to him as something that agrees with what he bears inside or what he has given rise to.

The greater his longing is for the grasping of the Will of the Light, and the more open he is to the impressions that bring to him the fruits of this longing, inwardly and outwardly, the more clearly he will once again hear that voice from within which has always been there, but which has over millennia been covered or coated (not suppressed) with the veil of the voice of his intellect, which is the earthbound product of his earthbound brain.

The person who inwardly does not bear the true desire to know this Will is like one who is not thirsty. He would not ask for water and would not truly appreciate it if it was given to him in such a state. It is simply not for him and cannot penetrate to him. He has not asked to know this Will; for the asking is done by the nature of the deep inner desiring. The true desire to know alone makes it possible for him to recognise that which can help him *know*. His reaction to that which comes to him along this path will express the earnestness of his desire to see. What he expresses along this upward path goes on to develop for him his future conditions, which must hold for him even more potential for awakening experiences, which allow him to see how he is to be as a human being on earth, and this will be further reflected in the nature of his thoughts, words and actions. He will become more and more open to what comes from above to help him along this path.

When he is able to draw from that which comes from above, and which therefore stands closer to the Light, he is able to transmit what is healthy and therefore develops in good form, just like the cell in the human body which has the right genetic code and which has not been compromised through an invasion by some alien species with some alien genetic code.

The rightly developing cell is also able to contribute to the right development of the human body in the same way as man can help bring beauty and perfection to his surroundings as he develops upwards, through the absorption of the guiding rays that come from above. These rays bear the pictures which, in being absorbed and put into practice on earth by man, gradually reveal to him through personal experience, and to the extent that his species is able to absorb, the true nature of the working of the Power that is the Will of God.

It can only be absorbed by man from within himself, as a consequence of his petitioning for the opportunity to do so through the nature of his inner attitude. Only the true desire to do what is good can form the basis for this kind of reception. Only this desire can form the petition for this kind of experience; because the currents that come from above are always lighter, less veiled and less burdened, producing pictures that are less dimmed and less distorted, and thus bringing about conditions that reveal more goodness in the just response to the sowing of the seed of goodness. It cannot be given to man from the outside; not by anyone.

If man fails to do this he, by default, draws currents from some other direction, which will always be inferior to what comes from above, akin to what happens when the machinery in the cell reads and interprets genetic codes other than those that are useful for the right human cell development. His perceptive antenna, so-to-speak, comes lower to the realm of his earth-bound thoughts, which make up his intellect. What he draws and transmits in this state would always be full of gaps and incomplete, thus wrong, because it would not take into consideration everything necessary for upward growth such as only what comes from above can deliver.

One can also imagine and come to experience personally that it is only that which comes from above which has the capacity to *pull* or *attract* upwards, but never that which comes from the side or from below! When the pull comes from above, then the necessary components needed for right formation come together in the most perfect and balanced way, presenting a kind of symmetry that is often associated with simple greatness. When the pull is from one side, however, that which comes together in the formation of the structure being created does so without such symmetry and balance; it is one-sided.

Man's dependence on his intellect is analogous to what happens in the picture provided above about the viral infection of the cell; only, of course, the consequences of the deviation are much more devastating and affect the very existence of the spirit which, as the real, *living* entity in man, is able, if it so wills, to consciously exist *eternally* following the completion of its *right* development in the several planes of the material world. Success in this depends on how he affects the different planes of matter in the course of this development. As a result of this man is able to affect the entire world of matter – the gross material earth as well as that which lies beyond it – through the way he attunes himself within.

But, sticking to this earth-plane for the moment, what the person so inclined as to have his volition directed mainly towards earthly matters draws to himself, in the form of earthly conditions, is just that which provides him with the opportunities to experience the fruits of the base seeds that unavoidably emanate from deep within him every moment. This is due to his self-imposed incapacity to draw down to himself guiding pictures which, in guiding him aright from above also pull him spiritually upwards closer to the Light.

In his pursuit of his narrow earthly goals he will express emotions that are not light and upbuilding, and which will reveal his incapacity to experience happiness in circumstances other than the ones in the narrow pictures that he holds within. He will express fear, anxiety, disappointment, greed, narrow-mindedness, distrust, one-sidedness, conceit, anger, and so on, and his earthly conditions will be put together accordingly, that is, in just those ways as will deliver to him mature fruits of the above-mentioned dark seeds.

These earthly conditions and what they deliver to him reflect the depravity and poverty of spirit that exist within him. The poverty and sickness of the inner man reflects the lack of that nourishment which can only come through the guiding pictures from above. The latter would bring about the expansion of the spirit, that inner welling-up with pure joy which arises from having come to some recognition, some form or degree of enlightenment, and which many a fortunate person would have experienced at one point in his earth-life or another. Man is kept from drawing these guiding pictures when he keeps his gaze focused downwards – only on matters that deal with earthly issues, needs, and desires. This is the consequence of an earthbound spiritual volition. What he draws in such a state must lead to chaos and destruction. It must reflect the severe narrow-mindedness and ignorance that is inherent in such a limited perception. And only the nature of the perception determines what forms and comes to one.

What comes out of him while his spirit is so encased and bound (due to the narrowness of his perception), and thus, contracted, stifled and languid, goes out as his spiritual *works* to influence others who may be susceptible. Since these works were formed with spiritual power, they also possess an attractive capacity, the strength of which will depend on the strength of the volition which led to their formation. They go on to attract similar deep inner feelings, thoughts and emotions from those who are of a similar nature, or those who are not strong enough to resist the tempting effect of such an ethereal pull of homogeneity.

These latter groups then go on to become stronger in their production of the same kinds of base emotions and associated forms as bring about fear, despair, narrow-mindedness, sordid sensuality, conceit, and so on, (just like the newly-infected cells in the analogy provided above do, as they produce viral proteins that aid viral replication and growth, so that viral particles spread further in the host body and infect more cells) to the detriment of the whole species of spirit that came into matter for the purpose of its development, as well as the development of the other cooperating creatures and the material worlds made available to it for this purpose.

As I have already mentioned, the forms produced under these conditions keep the gaze of the human volition directed downwards instead of upwards, so that what men attract and transmit to their earthly surroundings already bear, at the point of seed, the germ of destruction. They therefore encourage one so inclined to continue along the same fatal course.

It is also that which man bears within him, as a part of the cloaks that form around his spirit and form part of his soul, which determines the nature of the environment into which he is born in his next incarnation on earth, if he is fortunate enough now to still have such an opportunity. The re-embodiment or reincarnation of a soul, following a prior departure through earthly death, is only the entrance of the already existing soul into a newly formed physical body and environment, with its peculiar conditions, which suit perfectly and are homogeneous to the current nature of the incarnating soul. Such conditions and bodies are suited for what the spirit has to experience in the new lifetime on earth. Nothing of this process is an "accident". The similarities between aspects of the nature of the incoming spirit and those of his parents are only simply due to the fact that such parents had attracted a spirit with similar tendencies and inclinations, as well as burdens to redeem. He chooses the couple to which he is born through his nature.

People who, through their conviction, decide that only material things are of importance, will find themselves in those circumstances where *seeing* differently is very difficult. In fact, seeing differently is impossible for them if there has not been a prior change in their attitude, which alone could allow for it. In the meantime, they will see and move along a path that is homogeneous to the desires expressed with their prevailing inner attitudes.

Like the infected cells in the human body, these human beings tag themselves through what they harbor inside and what they emit, and through this also place themselves on particular paths, which lead them to definite ends that accord with the nature of what they have expressed as their desired experience – elimination from the possibility of being able in the future to produce works that could influence others. The targeting for destruction that happens with the infected cells is similar to the bringing together of like-minded spirits here on earth, in the final leg of the journey of maturation, so that they could make this last lap together, in blindness or in good sight, towards that end which they have shown appreciation for through their innermost desiring, whilst giving to each other various versions or forms of what they bear within.

Those who favour anger, greed, envy, narrow-mindedness, conceit, vanity, spiritual indolence, various forms of intolerance, fear and anxiety, will move together as a homogenous group and inflict on each other that which they bear within, in the various ways that they individually exhibit the various traits of these various intuitive forms. This will make the envious more envious, the greedy greedier, and the fearful even more fearful, as they receive through people of a like nature that which they have sown and continue to sow due to the nature that they carry within.

Those who have become able to see justice, lawfulness, perfection in the workings of the Laws of Creation, love in its true form, and those who have become able to give of themselves without expecting anything in return, that is, with a genuine desire to give in order to bring benefit to the other, will find themselves drawn together with similarly-minded individuals who will, in exhibiting their own particular natures, deliver to them only that which would accord with this lighter nature.

Their experiencing of these fruits would manifest in their seeing brighter and more hopeful conditions and environments, and also their becoming more able to truly *see* as human beings. These would have sown the seed of wanting to see more clearly, for with their seed they sow light, and the fruit of their seed would attract those conditions that would make this kind of seeing possible. Their ability to see would naturally influence what they emit on a continual basis. This would naturally mean a continual drawing of many more of such conditions that would continually lead them upwards, through personal recognitions, towards that realm where what is lighter resides. This will happen step by step, experience by experience, moment by moment, hour by hour, and day by day, in a natural course of development and according to the Law of natural development, which is governed by the Laws of Creation.

In this way, each person sees only what he has made himself capable of seeing, through the way he has attuned his inner self, which latter actually does the seeing, and which at the same time lays the foundation for what eventually develops ahead of him on his spiritual and earthly path. That this is the process through which the future condition of man on earth develops becomes clearer to the one who has become able to *see*. Through this he is able to *know* that what develops for him to experience in his future is dependent on how he feels deep within himself in the present, how he intuitively perceives and reacts. His approach to overcoming obstacles that he finds along his path, as he lives his life on earth, changes as a result of this recognition. He sees more clearly the beginning of the process that brings to him his physically tangible earthly fate. This he could not have seen when he remained blind to the goings-on outside of the earthly plane due to his previously earthbound way of thinking.

★ ★ ★

As the volition of men became more and more directed towards the pursuit of earthly power and influence, the world that formed around them grew darker and darker, because they did not provide the conditions on earth for the drawing down and absorption of light vibrations in the form of purer spiritual currents from lighter planes above. The darkness in question here is that which keeps the human spirit from truly seeing - from seeing the connection between sowing and reaping, seed and fruit, beginning and end, inner spiritual volition and physical, earthly manifestation.

When the human spirit does not see *aright* he acts blindly and in ignorance, and everything that emanates from him in this state must also be wrong and dark; must have a darkening or blinding effect on his surroundings. So, over time, man's ethereal and earthly environment developed wrongly, with a one-sided focus on what is earthly and what brings earthly gain, and without enough attention, if any at all, to the part of his existence that lies outside of the earthly gross material, and which is by far the greater part.

This is quite similar to what happens when the human cell has been successfully invaded by a virus and its protein-making machinery has been taken over by the virus. What is formed within the cell can no longer bring about the right development and maintenance of the cell. The structures, proteins, and other substances produced within the cell would be ones best suited for the production of more viruses. This task - the production of more viruses - becomes the primary task of the cell. It no longer admits of any other genetic code for the production of any other kind of protein but that which leads to the production of viral proteins. This happens in many of the cases because, with the introduction of the viral genetic material into the core of the cell, and the take-over of the protein-making machinery of the host cell, certain viral proteins are then produced upon the reading and decoding of the genetic material introduced by the virus, which then go on to inhibit the production of the host cell proteins.

Other proteins produced in this way further the replication of the viral genetic material and the production of proteins needed for the outer casings that house the genetic material of the virus. The more viral proteins are produced in the cell therefore, the more host cell protein production is suppressed. So, in order to take over the protein-production machinery of the cell for the purpose of making viral proteins, the production of human cell proteins is inhibited. This also means that the production or replication of host cell genetic material ceases.

What forms in the earthly and material environment of man takes on the likeness of the vibrations that he allows to pass through him. What is formed around him acts as a channel for the return-flow of similar currents to him. So, if he does not make his decisions with the desire to bring about goodness and light, then the structures that would arise as a consequence of his nature would encourage further deviation from goodness and light. So, as man forms oppressive conditions for himself through the way he is within, he strengthens, through what he forms, his connections to the source of more oppressive vibrations, thus ensuring the production of more of the same kinds of conditions.

He strengthens, through this, his connections to those worlds where dark thoughts and inner perceptions take on form. So, with his focus mainly on what will further his earthly influence and his ability to have and hold on to earthly power, man formed an earthly environment that narrowly focused on the attainment of this goal. His attention and, therefore, his ability to attract, were not directed to what lies higher than what is earthly.

Through this man cut himself off from the supply of spiritual currents, and thus from the flow of pure energy-forms. The darkness and loss of power that surrounded him took on the form of the educational, legal, governmental and commercial institutions that developed in his earthly surroundings. The world of art and entertainment that developed on earth also reflected the one-sided focus on the physical and the earthly, in a way that encouraged more of the same from him in various forms. He could not see what was at the core of the conditions that developed around him and also in faraway lands. He was focused on the pursuit of his earthly desires and goals, which did not require or allow enough time for the right consideration of anything else. His interpretations of the goings-on on earth were mainly based on his very limited understanding of the purpose of life on earth. This also meant that his reaction to them were just as superficial and could not address the cores of the issues that he faced. These cores, however, were formed through the way he was within.

He naturally could not see his own contribution to that which came to him through his earthly surroundings; either from another country through the news or through some form of entertainment, or from close by through personal experience.

The oppressive conditions in all nations, the moral decadence revealed through increasing expressions of sordid sensuality, debasing entertainment and the development of a morally-bankrupt social environment, all allowed for men's gaze to remain focused mainly on what is physical and earthly, so that they continued to nourish the aforementioned forms.

Trade, exchange, and general intercourse between men were based on deep inner feelings of fear, distrust and narrow self-interest. Fear of what earthly influence or material could be lost, distrust of his fellow man whom he considered a rival in the pursuit of his very narrow earthly goals and narrow self-interest, which are focused mainly on gain in the physical and earthly sense. This ensured that all of men's thinking was focused on and limited to the very narrowly-defined boundaries of what is earthly. And since man attracts currents from that realm where his attention is directed, he could only attract currents from the lowest and densest parts of Creation.

As mentioned earlier in this book, spirit particles become coated and veiled as they pass through the planes of Creation, from above downwards. The flow of these particles through Creation is at the same time the flow of energy through Creation. What is formed in the finer, lighter and higher planes in Creation is more beautiful and better put together than what forms in the lower planes. The higher, lighter planes above are more penetrable and sensitive to the Power of the Light than are those planes which are lower and therefore more distant from the Light.

The animating currents bear spiritual power and, in coursing through Creation, come together in the forms that we recognize, including the solar systems, the planets, the rocks, the trees, and so on. The more veiled these particles are, that is, the deeper they sink into the lower planes in Creation, the less beautiful what is formed will be in comparison to what is formed in the planes that lie higher. Therefore, when man restricts his capacity to attract, to perceive, to the lowly planes of the earth, he puts a strict limitation on the amount and quality of energy currents he is able to draw to himself. What he is then able to form with this inferior quality of energy currents must express or manifest the inferiority of the vibration of such currents.

So, when men limited themselves to perceptions within the range of what is earthly, they also ensured that only ugly conditions could arise and thrive on earth. Such conditions could only reflect the nature of the vibrations that led to their formation. With each thought, each word, and each visible action carried out by man in this state, he wove a thread of a particular color and vibration into the fabric of what formed for him to experience on earth. The resulting environment was one that allowed for only corresponding activities to thrive.

So, the collective work of men has for millennia permitted the flourishing and thriving of mainly what is dark and misleading. Just as happens in the case of an infected human cell where mainly or only viral proteins are produced; and just as suited man's earthbound volition, since it made it possible that only earthbound desiring thrived in the hearts of men. Out of this came all the evil that men now wish to run away from. They became slaves of their own desires, the true natures and consequences of which they could not see in their self-imposed spiritual blindness, which always goes together with conceit and narrow-mindedness. In such a state, mankind could not truly petition for help, because what emanated from deep within them expressed the desire for pain, hardship and destruction. With their thoughts and actions they sowed the seeds for these fruits and received them in great abundance.

They became prisoners of their own works. Help could only come to them from outside, from the Light. And when it was sent to them through prophets and *called* ones, these were ridiculed because what they brought was not recognized as advantageous by the intellect, to which a majority of men had made themselves subject. But without a change in their inner attitude, they could never become able to attract to themselves lighter and more favorable conditions in their ethereal and physical environments. Their spiritual blindness could not allow them to see the origins or beginnings of those conditions which, in many cases, they sought to change and improve upon. They were left with only physical efforts, which only expressed the one-sidedness and superficiality that they bore within. They remained bound to continually experience various forms of the same fates that they hoped to eradicate with physical or manmade laws.

But the intended help, and the help that was sent to men, was directed at the *inner part* of man, the core of which is his spirit. For it is there, at his core, that the change is needed. A change there, deep within him, must show itself in what forms around him, and in what he draws to himself as his fate. Without a change in his inner life, in the nature of his inner attitude, there could never be a change in what manifests outwardly for him. To change the outward forms through the passage of new man-made laws would be like putting a bandage over an open sore on the skin, which has only manifested as a symptom of some serious internal ailment. Sooner or later the presence of the disease within the body would manifest itself again in perhaps another form - on the surface.

Those who brought help to men in the different regions of the world could not remove the deficiencies within men simply by bringing the help. Men themselves had to *want* to accept the help, and had to act accordingly in order to attract, recognise and make use of the help. In other words, it had to be the volition of men to want to change inwardly in order to bring about different inward and outward conditions, and for them to be at all open to the help that was brought to them for this purpose. Without this inner desire they would perceive the help sent to them as antagonistic to their efforts towards the fulfillment of their true desires which, for the most part, involved the pursuit of earthly power and influence.

So it was that men fought against all bringers of help sent by the Light over millennia, as well as against the Son of God Himself, Who did not come to found a religion, nor did He come to preach to or educate only a group or specific segment of men, but Who came for the sake of all those who truly *desired* help, and who, through their inner attitudes and actions, proved capable of receiving it. The right inner attitude would always have as a part of its nature that humble openness that is ready to receive. Only one with such an attitude could be called a seeker for Truth.

All religions and all forms of the religions in existence on earth today have been formed by men, and as such, only manifest that which lies within those who hold them together. Many have arisen through men's attempts to grasp and interpret teachings that were at one time willed by God for delivery to men. But they have been taken through the mills formed by the narrow conceptions of men in the course of their transmission and interpretation, and no longer reflect just what was initially brought. The distorted forms in which the teachings exist and are passed on today only reflect the inner states of those who keep the various religions going.

If they had arisen or been formed at some point for the purpose of helping adherents find the right path to the knowledge of the Will of God, so that this Will could be abided by, this still does not make them the work of the Creator! They are the work of spiritual creatures which make use of the neutral Power of God in Creation for the formation of works that agree with their own volition. This volition of theirs could come closer to or move farther away from the Will of God, and would reflect this distance or closeness accordingly. It is left to man himself, this spiritual being in material cloak, to investigate for himself, in the course of his own personal experiencing, the true nature of his God! He will find help for this everywhere around him, because there is nothing that has come into being outside of the working of the Laws of Creation, which are the expressions of His Will in Creation, and as such, the gateway to a *knowing of* the nature of the Creator.

The Laws of Nature are the Will of God and show man the nature of the working of His Power. The closer one comes to acting in accordance with these Laws the better he would be able to read the Language of God in Creation. He would be lost if he decides to follow another guide. What is natural for the spirit, however, must lead it to greater spiritual maturity as it ascends upwards to its origin in the Spiritual Realm.

Everyone is capable of recognising this if it is his sincere desire to do so! He will come across precious stones here and there along his own path of experiencing, which will point to the right direction *for him*, as long as within him lies the desire for this. These precious stones would bring to him recognitions that would together form for him a picture of the working of the Power of the Light in Creation, in a way that makes this Will (the Power of God) known to him in a very personal way.

Only then would he be in a position to assess whether or not some teaching that he comes across bears *something* of the Truth, because he would have acquired the personal experiences that would make him capable of making such an assessment for himself. That is, he would have, through his experiences, become more open to the guiding impressions that would help him with such an assessment, which takes the form of an inner weighing and examining, and which does not require much time or effort, or any formal training.

But one can only weigh and examine where there is something of known weight and substance against which to measure. This knowledge, this known substance, can only be attained through personal experiencing.

The effort towards this goal will bring about the development of those gifts that he does not share with anyone else, and which are only brought to life when aligned with the life-sustaining stream of power currents from above. Such an alignment is only achieved when one adapts his thinking, speaking and acting to the upbuilding nature of the Laws of Creation. In the working-out of these Laws or Principles of Working, that which ennobles, enriches and nourishes is always maintained, further developed and lifted upwards; while that which disturbs, endangers, poisons, burdens, stifles or kills is always pushed downwards and allowed to go through disintegration, because it would have proved to be useless to the ever-ongoing upbuilding in Creation. As it is pushed downwards it is forced to occupy a narrower space. It becomes denser and more solidified or rigid, and its range of movement is narrowed to only a sinking downwards.

This is similar to what happens with the absorption of nutrients from digested food for the building-up of a healthy human body, and the passing-out of excreta, which would become toxic to the body if it were to remain in it for too long.

The Power that sustains and drives Creation is borne by spiritual currents. This is because the Power of God, Which is also the Will of God, is the Spirit of God. The effects of the Radiation of the Creative Spirit of God are what we experience as the Power of God, and we can recognize It in the Laws of Nature or Laws of Creation. These Laws cannot be separated from the physical laws that we live our lives by and upon which science thrives. No movement, not even the slightest stirring, can occur outside of their working. From the beginning and for all eternity they have been and shall remain the governing principle behind every happening. That is, every happening takes place according to the working of these Laws, which manifest the Will of God in Creation.

It is the effect of this working, carried by spiritual currents, which courses through Creation as animating energy. The continuous and uninterrupted flow of this energy current leads to the uninterrupted growth and expansion of the entire Creation, and to the welfare of all the creatures in it, which all benefit from the proceeds of this flow of energy currents from the Light through Creation, and back to the Light. In the same way as the flowing water of the stream or river is able to help maintain and increase fertility along the path of its course, and the flow of blood in the body is necessary for the distribution of vital substances for the proper growth and maintenance of the cells, tissues and organs of the body, and for the general well-being of the body as a whole.

Ultimately, the Laws of Creation work towards the right maintenance of the flow of necessary creative spiritual currents, and so does any creature that remains natural in its activities. For man to play his part in this process and not be a hindrance to it, he must become knowledgeable of the Laws of Creation and adapt himself to them. To do this he simply needs to develop what lies within him, which sank into the World of Matter as an undeveloped seed-germ, bearing within it all the abilities necessary for the fulfillment of its role as a developed spirit, one which is able to transmit creative energy currents in Creation.

It is the Will of his Maker that he does this, and he can only discover the workings of these Laws (which express this Will) and be encouraged to voluntarily heed them, when he experiences within him and also outside of him the unending and unchanging process of sowing and reaping, of the coming together of similar species or forms, and of the classification or stratification of these homogeneous species according to how closely they align themselves with these Laws; all of which reveal to him aspects of the inconceivable Love of God, Which shall eternally remain inseparable from His Will.

When he recognises the strictness of the working that always brings to a person that which he has sown as seed with his inner attitude, thoughts, words and deeds, and when he sees that what he gets is dependent on what he gives through his own attitude, thoughts and deeds, then he is encouraged to only put forth what is good.

When he does so, the effects of his corresponding works will always lead to his absorption of more spiritual currents from above, in accordance with the Law of Sowing and Reaping and the Law of the Attraction of Homogeneous Species. This is because he would thereby be expressing the desire to receive more of what he is giving, and to be more closely connected to whatever may be similar to what he is expressing. Such closer connection with, and increase in the flow of spiritual currents, must lead to the animating and bringing-together of the material substance around him in a correspondingly more beautiful manner, such as would also show itself in the way that he experiences the physical or earthly conditions that develop for him.

This will bring about the ennoblement of everything that he touches in his thoughts, with his words or also physically. Such ennoblement will be an expression of his being attracted upwards by stronger spiritual species. It will raise the entire plane on which he resides to a higher level – one which is closer to the Source of the power-bearing spiritual currents that he will be receiving more of, in accordance with the natural Law of Gravity. *This* will be natural for man, because he is of the spirit.

Due to the personal nature of his experiencing of the working of the natural Laws that govern Creation, that is, because the recognitions and impressions strike him at his spiritual core, he is left with deep impressions that cannot be easily shaken by forces from outside of him. In this way, he gains in conviction and matures spiritually. The process of spiritual growth and maturity leads to the increased movement and glowing of the spirit, and the step-by-step removal of the layers of denser coverings, which taint and distort man's perceptions of how things really work around him.

The attempt at being more conscious of the *true* nature of his inner and outer movements, as well as of the nature of the potential effects of the seeds sown with these movements, leads him to reap the fruit of increased consciousness regarding the nature of the working of the Laws that govern Creation – the Laws of Creation. This knowledge can only come to man from above. Such attempts at conscious movements and activity can only be made by the spirit of man, since only the spirit is mobile within itself and as such is able to move towards their realization. This kind of striving therefore requires, as well as aids, spiritual movement. Energy in the form of spiritual currents must therefore be drawn by the one who truly engages in this kind of activity. This makes it so that the drawing of currents of spirit and, as a result, of power, can be achieved by everyone on a continual basis in the several moments that make up the hours of the day.

Each layer or veil that is removed through this process allows him to see better the workings of the machinery of Creation. It reduces his exposure to the vibrations of conceit, narrow-mindedness, selfishness or egotism, spiritual ignorance, distrust, fear, and general denseness or coarseness, which lie lower, and connects him more firmly to those higher currents that instill more trust, confidence and conviction in the perfection of the Laws of Creation.

He exposes himself through this to different energy currents, which lead to his formation of different ethereal forms of intuitive perception, through which he pulls together magnetically for himself corresponding physical conditions. So, because his surroundings form according to how he *sees* spiritually, which is the same as the way he feels *deep within him*, the degree to which the clear perception of his spirit is veiled therefore affects the kind of energy currents that come through the correspond-ingly formed physical environment.

A narrow-minded person, for instance, will make his decisions based on his narrow-minded mindset, and would move along the path of narrow-mindedness in the way he thinks and speaks. What will form for him at the point of maturation of the seeds sown by him in the course of these actions will lead to his experiencing of even more nar-row-mindedness in its various forms, according to the degree to which he himself has been and remains narrow-minded.

The oppressive and painful consequences of this weighty attribute, which will come to him also through other narrow-minded people, will inflame his own narrow-mindedness and cause it to grow and develop so that it finds even more ways of becoming evident in his surroundings.

All of this will depend, of course, on the nature of his inner attitude at the time when he has to experience what has become ripe for him to reap, and on his response to it upon its impact on him.

It is the same with a person who feels, nourishes and therefore sows envy, as well as for the person who sows selflessness and true love for his fellowman. What he sees will aid in the development of the lens through which he sees it. The one who sows envy will extract and see from what has formed that which will cause the growth and development of the veil or lens of envy, while the one who sows courage and confidence in the perfect working of the Laws of Creation will see what will strengthen this perception of trust and confidence, of perfect Justice. And with the perception of confidence he is able to act more courageously and thus form better conditions for himself.

It is in this way that one who strives to know and abide by the Laws of Creation, and who therefore bears within him the earnest desire for this, recognizes that which strengthens this longing. What strengthens this longing also increases his confidence in their unfailing nature. What he experiences and sees through this longing causes the gradual peeling off from his spiritual core of the hindering layers of distorted conceptions, so that he sees more manifestations of this working in a manner that causes his confidence in its perfection to grow. He becomes convinced that these Laws always work in the same manner that they have consistently manifested in his experiencing, and will never change to a different way of working in the future. He trusts in this perfection completely.

This trust is needed by every person in order for him to be able at all to cultivate courage and conviction, as well as that steadfastness which will enable him to always think and act in accordance with what will bring goodness and spiritual maturity. Through the upright, beautiful and clear forms that result from this way of being, more spiritual currents will flow into the material surroundings of man, bringing with them more animating power from the Light. There will be less dimming of the intensity of this power because of the crystalline clarity and beauty of that which will be formed through the desire to act as true *human beings.*

The foothold that one who acts thus has in his environment is more solid, as a result, because he is more confident. He has discovered something that he has personally experienced to be trustworthy and reliable – the immovable and unchanging Laws of Creation. And because he emits confidence as a result of this discovery, he draws more confidence in return, in accordance with the Law of Reciprocal Action. For him, to draw more confidence means to go through conditions that will cause him to experience more confidence; for as he sows, (in this case, as he gives off the acquired confidence in his thinking, speaking and actions) so shall he reap, many times over!

To act with trust and confidence in the perfect working of this process requires the personal experiencing of it. It cannot come to man in any other way. It certainly cannot be handed to him by someone else or by any group. In fact, he could not become more confident in the perfection of this expression of the Will of God even if the Son of God Himself stood before him here on earth with the desire to have him see this perfection, if he himself did not harbor the earnest desire for it and greatly exert himself to see it, to feel it intuitively deep within him. He alone holds the key to its reception. It comes to him through the opening of himself through the right attunement of his inner attitude, just as happens when one tunes into the right frequency in order to receive vibrations from a particular radio station.

Only then could it become his, a part of his own inner make-up and nature, because then it would be imprinted on his spirit, on his living consciousness, and would cause it to change accordingly. Only this change could permit his right experiencing of it, because he would have become capable of drawing it to himself in the course of passing it on through his actions. He would have become capable of transmitting it, and it is this which makes him capable of drawing or receiving it in the first instance, and consequently receiving more of it.

Man must become able to recognise his own contribution to the conditions that have formed for him to experience, whether good or bad. He must come to the point of being able to see his own hand in it. Only then could he see the justice in what has come to him. Only then could he make the connection between seed and fruit and see the complete cycle of the happening.

When he has come to see, upon objective observation, that he has always contributed to everything that has come to him, has in fact drawn it to himself, and when his expanded view of this working also allows him to see his contributions even outside of or prior to his present earth-life, then he can also allow himself to admit of different pictures from the one that he presently holds onto so rigidly, the narrowness of which keeps him imprisoned, bound or destined to a definite and corresponding fate. Rigidly holding onto the old picture leads him to the nourishment of distrust, for he does not give himself the chance to test and investigate, and then to trust and become convinced through personal experience.

The developed distrust is directed first and foremost at the perfection of the Laws of Creation, because he has not striven to know them. He cannot fully trust what he does not know, and he cannot truly know what he has not fully experienced personally; *no matter who comes to tell him about it.* This distrust, like all the other attributes that he nourishes, good or bad, helps make up the ethereal cloaks that form around his always-pure spirit, affecting its radiance. The veiling effect that this brings about correspondingly affects the nature of his perception. What comes to him and what he puts out all have to pass through this veil that he has constructed and which, together with the spirit at the core, forms his soul.

So, he is distrustful of his fellowman and of his surroundings because he *fears* that something that is due to him *can*, and therefore, may be taken away or fail to reach him, because of someone else or someone else's actions. His distrust emerges from within him in several forms. With the right understanding of the Laws of Creation, however, he cannot harbor this fear, because he would be certain that the Law of Sowing and Reaping cannot allow for the reaping by anyone of something that he has not sown.

His discovery that he is responsible for what forms for him also gives him the incentive to try to be different within. The fruits of this change would allow him to develop the trust in the process of sowing and reaping, as it actually occurs with man. This will lead him to the feeling and sowing of that necessary confidence and conviction needed for the formation of a path that leads upwards.

This is the intended result of the help that has been sent to man time and again. With his confidence in something that he has experienced to be truly trustworthy, i.e., the perfect working of the Laws of Creation, which always brings to him that which he has caused to come into existence, he can then let go of all negative attitudes. For all the adverse conditions that men have had to live through, all the terrible happenings that fill the pages of the numerous history books, all the evil that has been expressed through men over the ages, have at their cores the misguided, wrong and therefore evil volitions of men as their animating factors.

These wrong volitions all stem from man's one-sided focus on what is earthly. They show themselves, in their variety, in the forms of hatred, fear, greed, envy, conceit, selfishness, distrust, love of comfort and ease, vanity, arrogance, spiritual ignorance, the rigid attachment to the physical, which shows itself in the sordid nature of present-day sensuality, the pursuit of earthly power and influence, and so on, all of which serve to keep man increasingly more focused mainly on earthly matters and desires. This also determined the nature of the form of energy currents that men made use of, and the world that they formed with such absorbed homogeneous currents.

Just as happens in a cell infected by viral particles, where the entire cell becomes a factory for the production and replication of viral proteins and genetic material, which are specific kinds of energy forms that allow for the passage-through of specific kinds of energy vibrations, the earth and its surrounding ethereal environment became the workshop for dark forms, in service to the Darkness, which worked on earth through men's narrow and limited perceptions.

Only what served the Darkness thrived for ages. The formed conceptions about the nature of the Working of God on earth and beyond were not excluded from this.

Everything was wrong and served the Darkness. These wrongly developed conceptions promoted the greater multiplication of wrong attitudes and emotions, which led to the formation of correspondingly wrong and misleading earthly environments. The formation of the wrong conceptions can be seen as the misuse of power currents in the generation of wrongly-put-together forms, the distorted natures of which could only allow for the transmission of what was correspondingly distorted. The experiencing by man of this distortion is in the form of the pain and misery that he feels when he has to taste of the fruit of his volition, his thoughts, words and actions.

It is not that two powers existed; with God's on one side and that of some other dark entity on the other. But there was and has always been one Power which drives everything in Creation. There will also always only be one Power for all eternity! It is only that very far away, unimaginable distances from the Light Itself, from God, the pressure of the Radiation of the Light slackened (due to this humanly unimaginable distance), *allowing for* a cooling off of its temperature, and for the *possibility* of the existence of movements or vibrations that did not lead to ideal combinations and developments of forms, with the absorption and use of this power of God by human spirits.

The conditions allowed for the *possibility* of a deviation from the path of the Will of the Light, but it was the direction of the volition of men that determined the nature of what formed in such distant parts. The deviation did not have to happen, and ideal conditions could still, even at such a distance from the Light as they were, have been arrived at. It is just that the possibility of a different direction, due to the less intense effect of the Radiation of the Light at that distance, and the associated reduced magnetic pull of said Radiation, existed as part of the nature of the region. The possibility for man to choose a path that is different from what is willed by God, that is, what builds upwards and encourages ascent, was therefore a characteristic of the region in which he was to mature and grow strong, through tasting and experiencing, through the process of sowing and reaping.

Here, he was to develop through personally experiencing the consequences of decisions, thus through tasting the fruits of various seeds, in order to become convinced and certain of the right path to follow; that the path that leads to greater consciousness and to upward spiritual development is the one that pulls everything else together in the most beautiful way.

But even here, as also in every part of Creation, the Will of the Light, Which is the Power of the Light, and Which causes fruit to develop according to the seed sown, still prevails without the slightest change. In the course of this happening, homogeneous species are brought together and similarly weighted substances, forms, species and conceptions gravitate to the same level and world. There, they experience similar fates, because they are affected by the same environmental forces. In the perfect, that is, unchanging working-out of the Law that makes this happen everywhere, one is able to perceive and understand the Language of God, wherever he may find himself.

Men had the free will to choose how they wished to direct their ability to produce forms and effects. Had they maintained the right connection with the Light and the streams of spiritual currents that flowed into Creation from It, they would have caused this part of Creation as well to become aglow and to be animated enough to allow for no wrong vibrations or movements and, therefore, for no wrong or distorted combinations in the course of developments and in the generation of forms. They would have participated in the spread of light through their conscious service to the Volition: Let There Be Light!

But they used the power from the Light to form their material environments wrongly, and the pressure and pain that ensued from this was the fruit they had to reap, in strict accordance with the working of the same one Power which, in its effect, will always return to the sower the kind of seed that he has sown.

★   ★   ★

Lucifer was an Archangel sent to help with the development of the spirit seed-germs that had developed the urge to mature to self-consciousness, and which had become sunken into matter for this purpose; a process which would include their thorough knowledge of the Laws of Creation, and which would require for this purpose the development of the abilities which already lay latent within them.

Coming from the Divine Realm, outside of Creation, he was to

draw out with his correspondingly greater capacity to attract, the volition for what is good from the fledgling seed-germs, which had become
conscious of their existence, but which had not yet become self-conscious and mature, and were at risk of stagnating in their movements and
allowing their volition to sink to lower and darker realms. The sinking of
the volition would mean the drawing to themselves of correspondingly
low and dark conditions. On earth, he was to help men with the right
use of the material tool – the intellect – in the transmission of the radiations from above into correspondingly light earthly products.

The immense distance from the Source of all animation allowed for
the possibility of the developing spiritual creatures in Gross Matter to
stagnate in their efforts. Stagnation, if not immediately helped, leads to
a fall, to disintegration of what has been formed. It is the same with a
bird that has gained some height in flight and which then stops flapping
its wings. If it does not resume the flapping of its wings soon enough it
will lose the height gained as it falls lower, and it could even lose its life
or the possibility of ever flying again depending on the nature of the fall.

Coming from outside of Creation, it was the volition of the Archangel that came down in the form of the "Lucifer" we speak and hear
about. The Archangel himself could not be in Creation and in the World
of Matter because his origin in the Divine Realm cannot allow for this.
Only a part of him could come into Creation, which is outside of and
below the Divine Realm, his origin. The descent into matter of the
Divine being itself is as improbable as the Sun coming down and being
situated in a part of the earth. But the rays of the Sun do come down
to the earth, and we speak of these rays and their effects as the Sun. It is
the volition of the Archangel alone that is and was able to come down,
to exert an influence on that which resided in Creation, and which had
taken on form outside of the Divine Realm.

This volition, which can be considered as a part of the Archangel in the Divine Realm, took on form as a personality and bore the desire to help the developing spirit-germs. Since it was sent out by the Light, behind it worked the Power of the Light. In the Divine Realm, its origin, the actions of the Archangel is one with the Will of God, but this changed at those distances from the Light where there had been a cooling off of the intensity of the radiation of the Light due to a slackening in the pressure. This volition, which is like a ray from the Archangel in the Divine Realm, adopted a different nature in the course of working at great distances from its origin. The ray was thus dimmed, and through this became distorted and altered. As already mentioned, it was also at such a great distance – the furthest from the Light – that the human spirits, which left as spirit-germs, were gradually developing.

The part of the Archangel sent out to help in Creation, due to the change which had taken place in it, became increasingly separated from the Will of God, which meant that it developed its own volition which no longer agreed with the strict working of the Laws of Creation, which latter express the Will of God. There is no possibility of this happening in the Divine Realm, where the intensity of the Radiation of God is such as can only allow for a vibration which strictly accords with His Will.

This intensity is reduced as the radiation travels further away from the Light Itself into great distances, unimaginable to the human spirit. With the decrease in intensity comes the splitting of the radiations into different directions, a dispersal which is due to a decrease in the temperature and the magnetic and holding pressure. The intense magnetic pressure in the environment of the Divine Realm cannot allow for the existence of a volition or a way of working that is separate or different from that of the Will of God. Only at distances unimaginable to the human spirit can a change occur and the possibility of this splitting and dispersal, or separation, come about!

At the point where Lucifer was no longer in strict accord with the Will of the Light, he became the strongest influence which pulled susceptible creatures away from the Way of the Light. This is because he retained the capacity to attract, which, originating in a much higher sphere than the human spirit, made him the strongest *spirit* in the region. Being the strongest spirit meant that his volition had the strongest ability to attract and thus, to have influence. And it was to this wrong influence that those weak and developing human spirits, which bore within them their own capacity to attract and form, fell.

The Principle of Temptation, which came to him while he was so far from the Light, was lacking in Divine Love, which would have been more patient with the still weak and developing mankind and helped them avoid falling. His impatience with the weaknesses that they expressed infuriated him and caused him to be even more impatient with men, and to move further away from transmitting what would help them overcome their weaknesses and ascend, as he transmitted through his *new* nature that which lured and tempted men away from the right path. What he expressed in this state went on to influence mankind in a negative way. And since he continued along this path, according to the natural Law of development, what was taking on form in the World of Matter through men continued to develop into what would cause him to give off a reaction that was wrong and downward-tending.

Those men who could resist this pull were stronger in the end, but many succumbed to the tempting radiations and lost the firm connection with guidance from the Light. They were lured to pay greater attention to earthly matters and concerns. Their focus became mainly directed at their earthly surroundings and what, in their view, would bring them earthly benefit.

But mankind did not have to fall to the influence of Lucifer.

Due to the unique position of the earth in the World of Matter, they stood, as it were, at a point where they could either be lifted upwards or be dragged downwards, depending on which direction they chose through the way in which they made decisions in the moments of the hours of their days. One step in either direction brought to them reinforcements that encouraged them along *that* chosen direction, and made it that much more difficult to go in the opposite direction.

Mankind would not have fallen had they not themselves deviated from listening to and heeding their pure intuitive perceptions, which is the same as their *inner voices*. They could not be made to do what their volition had not been inclined towards, for the direction of man's desiring (his innermost, as yet mostly unconscious stirrings) is what determines what forms for him in his future. Lucifer's influence could only incite or lure them away from the right path, through tempting them to keep their focus on earthly matters, and on such a low plane as would make it impossible for them to perceive aright the pure intuitive perception, which *always* points in the right direction as it seeks to pull men upwards.

When one observes animals in one's environment, one would find that they are mostly, if not always, driven by the urge to satisfy some basic material or physical instinct. The urge to feed, survive, to satisfy the pure animal sexual instinct and care for and protect the offspring that often result from the latter, generally moves animals towards the actions and behaviors that we ascribe to them. They act naturally when they focus on those needs, on their satisfaction, for that is the highest to which they can attain. In excelling in such goals they help maintain the movement and vitality that is necessary for upward development on earth.

The sexual instinct is active in the drawing together of the positive and feminine parts of the species of animals, which is necessary for propagation, growth and survival of the species. The above-mentioned pure animal instincts are necessary for the maintenance of vitality and balance in the natural environment of the earth. Animals need not strive towards a higher goal than the fulfillment of these natural instincts in order to have played their vital roles. The maintenance of animation and movement within the natural environment of the earth is their basic role. It could happen, however, that some animals could serve in additional forms through the service that they provide men.

The human spirit in man, being spiritual, has a goal which stands much higher, the attainment and satisfaction of which is what is natural for man. Each person would have to see how he has to attain to this goal for himself, for the path each has to take towards it is different from that of any other's.

But without exception all men fail in this regard when they do not recognize in which direction they are to channel their efforts and their energy in order to express, and therefore, engage in what is *natural* for the human spirit. The direction of their volition determines the nature of their future experience, since it dictates the form of their everyday earthly conditions, and the worlds into which the further developments of these conditions take them. For this reason, men should always be striving to know better the world around them and the reason for their being in it. They would, in so doing, avoid the unfavourable and often oppressive conditions that only manifest as expressions of their deviation from what is natural for them, and what brings peace and joy. They would be able to achieve this by recognising the effects of their inner attitudes on their surroundings.

When a man makes this effort he will become able to always see more each day, if not each hour, than he had previously been able to see of what he is capable of as a creature of spirit. But by enticing woman to view motherhood as the highest and most valuable goal for her, Lucifer tempted or invited woman to look upon those steps towards attaining to this position more highly than those involved in the development and maturation of her spirit, her real self. He lured her to strive towards a much lower goal, which required a different kind of attitude than would be necessary for the striving towards the right goal.

With this he invited her, through the tempting vibration, to lower and confine her spiritual gaze, which is the same thing as to cut herself off from the spiritual currents that come from the homogeneous spiritual world above. With this she also lost the ability to receive clear guidance through the spiritual pictures of happenings and forms in the spiritual realm. By succumbing to this temptation woman lowered her gaze to focus mainly on matters that dealt with her being able to become a mother. So she concerned herself more closely with becoming chosen by man for procreation, *which involved sexual intercourse.*

She therefore one-sidedly placed a lot of focus on the enhancement of her physical appearance for the purpose of attracting a man. The possession of a *desirable* physical form and the maintenance of sufficient capacity to draw the attention or gaze of the man rose to the highest of positions in the priorities of many a woman. The desire to attain to these goals altered the focus of her volition and consequently influenced in a corresponding way the manner in which she made use of her natural gifts as a spiritual being. The subject of her focus, which was at the same time the core of her volition, became manifest in corresponding form in her ethereal and physical surroundings. It shaped the nature or direction of development of her surroundings.

Her capacity to charm and influence the man upwards was dragged down low for the purpose of physically seducing him, consciously and not so consciously. This helped aggravate the sexual instinct in man, as well as his desire to accumulate wealth for the purpose of attracting and keeping the woman; a desire which, at a more innocent time, had taken on form as the pure desire to nourish his body and provide material needs and protection for his family and his environment. In its right form this desire would have led to the right development of man and his material environment.

The sexual instinct was one-sidedly overdeveloped as a consequence of the thoughts of men being heavily focused on sexual intercourse with women who, in their intuitive perceptions, had mainly generated attracting ethereal forms that could no longer help man upwards due to their earthward-directed motivating cores, but which stimulated only what strove for earthly interaction and satisfaction, which naturally strove downwards. Men grew to mainly *see* and seek the qualities in women that agreed with this growing urge, instead of maturing to see the higher qualities that they bore, and which were necessary in their well-developed forms for the spiritual growth and maturity of all mankind.

The thoughts and actions regarding sexual intercourse with a woman no longer were restrained within the context where there was already existing spiritual harmony between the man and woman in question; whereby the thoughts, words and physical actions were only the natural gross material manifestations of what had already taken on form in higher spheres due to this upbuilding spiritual coming together of harmonious souls. The requirement for this prerequisite was no longer necessary and became lost in the new and dark environment in which the sexual instinct became ruler instead of remaining subject to the higher spiritual.

Through this unnatural switch man placed himself under the control of the sexual instinct, instead of controlling it through ensuring a spiritual, and thus, noble inner attitude prior to allowing for the formation of thoughts and actions of a sensual nature directed at the woman. His heavier focus on the physical part altered the natural order of things for him and placed him on the path to experiencing the natural consequences of such a distortion. With the currents meant for the spirit he nourished the growths of all manner of distorted forms through this.

He, as spirit, became subjugated through his own will to the physical sexual instinct, and became enslaved by it. The manifestation of this condition of slavery can be easily recognised by anyone who cares to look. There is nothing that it has not affected negatively, for everything has suffered through man's one-sided focus on what is earthly and physical. One can easily perceive the threads from this with which the Darkness furthers, through men, the advancement of the complete absorption of this part of Creation into the Realm of Darkness.

What was drawn out of men in this state encouraged and led to more of the same corrosive development within women. The corresponding intuitive perceptions and thoughts from them, directed at women, had the effect of keeping the then susceptible, open and unguarded women more and more firmly on the path towards maintaining this downward trend in the development of mankind. She, in return, and as the bridge for everything that comes to mankind, delivered the only kind of currents that could travel along such a dark and misleading path as was formed through this kind of activity. Only that which allowed for its continued existence, growth and development was therefore transmitted and put into earthly form through woman.

Through this attitude woman lost her protection and fell. But she could not fall without taking with her the masculine part of her species, which needed her for the reception of higher vibrations from above. She set the standard that men have followed and given all kinds of twists and formations to. The mere appearance of woman, while retaining this inner attitude, could not but draw from men that which agreed with the low plane to which she directed her attention – the gross material physical. In this part, where the sexual instinct then ruled, the mere appearance of woman tempted man to sin, for the distortion which she bore within could not keep from being expressed in everything that she did. This included her mode of dressing, walking, talking, interaction with others and the worlds into which she allowed herself to enter, physically as well as in her thoughts and intuitive perceiving.

He would have to put up a lot of effort to keep down the urge to think thoughts of a base nature regarding the woman in her presence or when he sees her image. But the strength required for this lies in the knowledge of the further and down-the-road implications of such base thinking and feeling. In the world that had become so darkened that the over-developed sexual instinct could be found at the centre of most, if not all issues, man found little reason to struggle against its debasing pull. With the passage of time he gave in to it more and more, until he could no longer detect anything wrong in the decadence that lay around him. In such a state he was happy to *let himself go*, just like woman had let herself go. This was a fruit of the Lucifer Principle of Temptation. It was then being propagated by men through their thoughts speech and actions.

The energy currents accessible to men in such a state could only be used to form distortions of what should be. So the conceptions of love, help, beauty, power, strength, justice, balance, governance, trade and so on, have developed so far in the wrong direction that man can no longer recognise the true or ideal forms of these conceptions. The denseness of the corresponding creations by men has caused the earth to sink even further from the Light. The inability to see clearly the Will of the Light and rightly understand concepts is an expression of mankind's density and their distance from the Light. So men have clung tenaciously, over time, to the idea of only concerning themselves with what they can see and hear physically and, with the power of the spiritual volition, have over-cultivated everything physical and earthly.

The exaggeration of the physical instincts led to their burgeoned growth and caused them to become the determining factors for the thoughts and actions of most men. They did not have the desire to know what could lead to their inner development, because their focus was drawn off in the opposite direction. They could only still clearly hear those cues that helped them along their chosen paths. And these became louder with each passing hour. One step led in the wrong direction and the next one took them even further down that path. With each step in the wrong direction, into a denser, more calcified world, it became more difficult to perceive and to consider anything of the spirit. The conceptions became more rigid and less subject to change and improvement. Thus mankind stiffened, hardened and sank.

They therefore not only became like animals, considering only what satisfied their physical needs, but sank even below animals, because they could not stop at just acting naturally in the realm suited for animals. With the animals the instincts were satisfied in innocence, but with men, since they were not rising to their natural place where *self-consciousness* is natural, satisfaction of the same instincts, with the wrong sense of priority associated with it, went together with a debasement and distortion of pure concepts. In such dense worlds they could not avoid forming what was wrong. They could only form what was good and right if they were striving upwards, towards the Source of the animating pure currents of spirit, towards what is homogeneous to spirit, towards what is spiritual.

They burdened themselves with guilt in the process of their one-sided pursuits, because the reasons for their actions were not for the purpose of bringing pure spiritual currents down to earth and spreading light. They did not reach so high in their striving and so could not draw such currents; did not want to. Greed, distrust, fear, sexual lust, narrow-mindedness and superficiality drove many an action within man and therefore were the seeds he sowed in the course of his interactions with others in such a darkened state. Nothing else was possible. These sown seeds developed naturally into corresponding fruits, ethereally and also physically. Such base reasons for men's actions were the volitions that developed, gathered strength and came back to men in the forms of the ethereal, psychic and physical conditions that they had to live through. The conditions that formed encouraged them to feel more of the base attitudes and emotions, and to simultaneously produce more corresponding forms, to the detriment of their natural development.

So, the desiring of mankind grew and developed, as does everything else in the material world, except that for man it drew him in the opposite direction from that which is natural for him. His capacity to attract substances around him and form his volition with those substances could not be stopped or changed, even if he formed with them what entangled him in a world that was dark and increasingly impervious to light rays. By directing this capacity one-sidedly on the physical, he over-developed the basic physical instincts for sexual intercourse (the sexual instinct) and for the acquisition of material resources or wealth for the upkeep of his physical body. This grew *naturally* out of the over-development of the intellect, which is charged with dealing with what is earthly. The resultant increased focus on what is earthly aggravated the one-sided overdevelopment of the intellect produced by the human brain.

The sordid sensual environment that has blossomed over time on earth, and which today is showing its ripened fruits in all their varieties, and the greed that cannot be separated from a world so coarsely put together, can be clearly observed by anyone without any real effort. The very fabric of the time has been woven with them by man.

These instincts, in their lob-sided, and therefore, unnatural forms became rulers over him, and the determinants for his thinking, speaking and acting. Through these unnatural formations in the intuitive perceiving and thinking of man, dark currents could then very easily flow and generate corresponding forms and effects on earth and in the entire World of Matter. This went together with the fact that the souls, which alone could come to earth through earth-women, had to also be just as dark as the women and their environment had become. They populated the earth from darker and lower regions of matter.

Had a bridge not been lowered to such dark realms through the coarsening of woman, it would have been impossible for the souls therein to incarnate on earth. They would have had to first go through the necessary experiences in such realms that would make them change and yearn for a better environment, and thus develop the volition for incarnation on a plane such as this earth would have been had it not been dragged down. That would have been the natural process for their incarnation upon the earth. They would have then become naturally capable of participating in the upward development already taking place on earth through its upward-striving inhabitants. They would not have come with the volition to sink it, as is the case with every soul that does not have the desire for what builds upwards.

Darkening the earth at the same time brought about a lowering of the bridge for the influx of such souls, because the earth became more homogeneous with such dark realms and a natural connection was therefore automatically formed. The souls that came to the earth plane through this bridge formed part of the energy force that mankind had chosen to fill his environment with. With the sinking of woman the entire World of Matter was placed in jeopardy. Some parts of it, including this earth, actually became parts of the regions of Darkness. So it happened that here on earth, for a long time, the Darkness had a stronger influence than the Light.

By valuing the satisfaction of their earthly concerns over heeding the Inner Voice, which brought guidance to them from above, they placed themselves on tracks that led to different destinations from the ones that were prescribed for them if they were to successfully develop self-consciousness as matured human spirits. The path that they placed themselves on led them further away from being able to see clearly the working of the Laws of Creation, which manifests and makes clear on each plane of Creation the Will of the Creator. The path led them towards a greater unwillingness to concern themselves with and know the Will of their Maker. They therefore never became able to carry out this Will through their activities so that they could, through this, form a world that allowed for Its clearer perception.

Not being able to see the simple greatness of this working, and not being able to recognise its unchanging nature and, thus, its perfection, men, with their indolent and therefore not-expanding spirits, could not develop any trust in it. Increasingly they favored only what they could see and sense physically, and lost the ability to form a link to higher and finer spheres. As already mentioned above, whatever can be seen or sensed with the physical senses is only able to show the smallest and final stages of all developments, and so cannot reveal the full picture of the sowing and reaping involved in them.

The *lack of trust,* which man bore within him regarding the perfection of this working, formed around his spirit, as a part of his soul, his inner life, and came through also in the physical with regards to his relations with his fellowmen and his physical surroundings. He, for instance, could not *trust* that he had influence over the nature of what came across his path for his experiencing. Not being able to experience the strict working of the Law of Sowing and Reaping caused him to look outside of himself for the causes of the things and conditions that came to him. His distrust for his fellow man grew, and his fear that he could lose something that he valued to the latter added to this. Everything that grew out of this one-sided view of man's, such as the forms of fear, hatred and envy, brought destructive currents with it, because it always belonged to the transient world, which shall eternally remain subject to disintegration after a period of development, and could never take on the characteristics of the spirit, which could be allowed to exist for eternity in the Eternal Kingdom of the Holy Spirit, the Spirit of Truth, the Spirit of God.

This was a derailment that bound the developing human spirit to the lowly planes of Creation, to the environment of the earth. This is because man could only satisfy his base desires here on earth or close to it. All that was formed with the ensuing current of lowly-vibrating particles could only further and maintain what was equally low and inferior, distorted. Gradually, all knowledge and memory of the previously experienced happenings outside of what was earthly faded and became lost. They turned into fables and fairy tales, which were not to be taken seriously by anyone who wished to be taken seriously.

Without knowledge of the greater part of the happenings to which they were connected, however, men went on to develop their wrong conceptions about everything and went on to make wrong and entangling decisions based on these wrong and narrow conceptions. They continually formed a prison for themselves, which they had to share with the living, torturous formations that were the fruits of their one-sided dependence and reliance upon the earthbound intellect. Being so one-sidedly cultivated and animated, the intellect (which can only make contact and deal with what is earthly, with the desire to further it) became the channel for the transmission of the energy of imbalance and one-sidedness to the earthly environment, in service to the Darkness, whose very nature stands in opposition to the Light, Whose Will is Itself Balance, Justice.

It is not that Lucifer has his power and God His, it is simply that Lucifer at first, due to the great distance from the Light, was able to apply or use this one power that he has access to, wrongly, and, in reaping the consequence, became even more separated from the Light and even more inclined towards further distorting the use of this power as he sank and, with his greater power of attraction, due to his much higher origin, becoming able to serve as an opposing influence to the upbuilding work of the Light here in the lowest part of Creation. He is the only one who could naturally have deserved the designation "Antichrist", because the effects of his works naturally lead away from the intended goal of Christ for human spirits.

When man begins to consider moving in a particular direction within himself, he already begins to draw to himself the conditions that would make this possible. He sends out the petition for this with his volition, and then with his thoughts, which form afterwards. In the physically tangible environment of the earth, the effects of this stirring already become manifest in the vibrations of those particles that cannot be seen with the naked eye, but which scientists already know to exist and are studying in greater detail today.

"Small causes, great effects" is a saying that aptly describes what happens when the volition of man first makes impact on the physical surroundings of the earth. These vibrating particles, which are many times more mobile than the more rigid forms that we can see, are in constant change due to the change that is always going on within man as he transmits the radiations coursing through the Universe that he is a part of. All that is connected with him constantly moves and rearranges itself to suite his inner attitude at any given time, through constant formation and dissolution. It wishes to form itself according to this attitude, and it is in the process of doing so that it forms for man the path that leads to his experiencing of what agrees with that particular attitude, after it has combined with other similar forms to give to man many more times the seed that he sowed. In other words, the conditions that come together physically for man to experience as fruit of his inner stirrings form for him a sphere or a world of a corresponding nature.

The human spirit that is the core of man responds to his environment by expressing volition, an inner desire which, in many cases, is an unconscious one. As already mentioned earlier, this takes on a form that accords with the nature of the volition, in a plane or world in matter the substance of which is much finer than that of the gross material earth. The developed form goes on to influence the nature of his thoughts, which also have their corresponding forms in a different plane that is of a coarser, denser nature than the world of the forms of his volition or intuitive perception. The words that he speaks in connection with this happening are formed according to the formed thoughts, which strive to carry out the volition or desire that first took on form as the human spirit's reaction to the happening or vibration.

So, a person could feel fear deeply within him, and it is this that he then spreads through the process that I have described, as the deep stirring of his spirit, the activity of which he is in many cases unconscious of. The mere perception of fear in this manner sets off (if this is not halted) the process of forming for him a link to the world where fear thrives and from which he receives even more stimulus for its expression, and also contributes to what forms for him in all the planes of the material world to which he is connected through the finer cloaks that he wears within him, around his spirit.

Through the forms of his fears he also links himself to others who may be inclined to feel the fears that he is susceptible to, and encourages them with the currents that he draws from homogeneous worlds of fear to feel even more fear and thus to grow or develop in this regard. Such people could then contribute to the development of different forms that are based on fear, to the degree that they have absorbed the currents of fear. What actions they carry out in their intuitive perceiving, their thinking and their acting will therefore be born of fear and would lead to the induction of fear in those whom such actions are able to affect.

On earth the formation of what agrees with this perception begins at levels so fine that man is not able to detect them with his available devices. But they already start coming together and forming for him a path that leads to the fate that he has expressed the *desire* for — the fate of more fear.

I already mentioned at the beginning of this work how the nature of the inner attitude of man has an effect on the way that the veiled energy-particles that form the most basic substances (sub-atomic and atomic substances) here on earth combine. The nature of the combinations depends on the nature of the energy force fields provided by man through the state of his inner attitude. Like the effect of a magnet in the midst of iron fillings, the formations at such basic levels take on the form of the inner nature of man. They combine in such a way as agrees with his volition, whether this volition or attitude leads to what is good or to what is bad. This happens in stages, from one moment to another, with each happening in each stage depending on the exact overall nature of the kind of energy-forms in existence to contribute its effects. Through this the formed structure assumes a particular resonance, which is able to change again as soon as a different vibration is introduced into it through a change in the volition of man. The nature of the resonance determines the nature of the bonds formed or connections made, and the forms developed as a consequence of such combinations.

In this way the earthly surroundings of man also develop according to what corresponds to the nature of his inner being. As he lives through what has formed for him as his physical and psychic conditions here on earth, he experiences the true nature of what he has put together and caused to become animated. These include the nature of the family unit, education and justice systems in the various nations, systems of government and leadership, the prevailing attitudes towards life and towards the understanding of the reason for our being, and so on. Everything is distorted or wrongly formed to the degree that the inner life of man exhibits one-sidedness, narrow-mindedness, fear, greed, distrust, hatred, conceit, vanity, superficiality, spiritual indolence and ignorance, lustfulness and sordid sensuality, all of which keep the focus of man on what is earthly, so that it draws only correspondingly dense and low energy currents, which go on to form only what transmits light dimly.

In such a state it is impossible to make the right sense of what comes to man from above. It is impossible for him to receive it in the form that is helpful to him. Everything is passed through the veil or filter of the network of threads and forms that weave cloaks for the spirit, through which it experiences its surroundings. What then emanates from the thus-veiled spirit goes on to sustain the attitudes which I have listed above, so that it keeps men sowing such seeds as will bring to man similar fruits to those listed above. So the radiations that come down to the human spirit on earth are diverted into ugly forms and kept from returning upwards in a natural upbuilding cycle. Such a cycle is necessary for the maintenance and furthering of Creation.

Through participating actively in the production and maintenance of said forms, man made himself a willing tool of the Darkness and carried out in finer detail the effects of the wrong *Principle of Temptation* of Lucifer, which at first the latter sought to use to weed out weak human spirits, but which, in lacking love and balance brought great devastation in its wake. It led down a path that could only develop into the state of utter darkness that everyone is able to recognise now, if he so wills.

To be tempted is to be lured into a particular world within which one then uses the above described capacities of the spirit to increase the prevalent forms of that world, and thus perpetuate the happenings in it in his own particular way. Once in that world, only what is of that world is animated, because the spirit goes into that world bearing within itself the capacity to draw animating currents into said world.

As soon as man has stepped in the direction to which he is being pulled by the tempting factor, the next steps in that direction become easier and follow the process of natural development.

Natural development is governed by the Laws of Nature, which have also been presented here as the Laws of Creation. According to the Law of Reciprocal Action, whatever one sows that he reaps, many times over. To move in a particular direction with regards to the state of one's inner attitude, and therefore, one's volition, is to sow the seed of wanting more of that which corresponds with the seed. The true and quite revealing nature of this working can only be really discovered by that person who earnestly and without reservations, strives to experience it in his own life, as objectively as he can (even if he at first begins by observing those around him). So, in developing onwards only what agrees with the nature of the seed comes in the successive stages of development, as long as the same kind of volition is maintained.

The Law of Attraction of Homogeneous Species, which is hinted at with the saying "birds of a feather flock together" and "like father like son", also causes the further development of the situation to agree in essence with the true nature of the seed sown with the onset of movement in a particular direction. According to the Law of Gravity, the height or depth to which the one connected with the happening is taken, as he proceeds in the initial direction, together with the corresponding change (upwards or downwards) in the levels or capacities of perception and clear-sightedness, will depend on the quality of the sown seed with regards to its denseness or lightness.

What tends towards evil, oppression and harm will always lead to coarser, baser, and more oppressive conditions. It will lead to increased darkness with regards to one's being able to see and know more, and thus to act better. The reverse is the case with a step towards bringing to life what is good. The latter will bring the one concerned into contact with that environment that will fire up even more within him the volition to do what is good. This means that the one concerned will experience such goodness as will inspire him even further along the path towards sowing and reaping more of the same. Everything along this path will be so configured as to further draw out this quality of volition from him. Even if at first the happenings serve to help him, through *unfavourable* conditions, to adjust his inner attitude in the right way in order for him to perceive more clearly the way that leads to peace and joy.

In the same way as the developments that become physically tangible to us begin in the finer substances of this earth - those being the bridges or points of first impact of the approaching radiations - the *finer part* of the developing human species on earth and in matter also serves as the bridge for what impacts mankind.

So it happened that the woman was the first to be seduced by the tempting factor inherent in the Dark Volition of Lucifer. She was the one that was approached, so to speak, in order to induce mankind to take a wrong turn, for she held the key through her finer nature to the steering of the volition of her species either upwards or downwards. Whichever direction she allowed herself to be swayed towards would show itself also in the activity, direction, and thus, nature of the volition of the coarser, denser and more visible part of the species – the masculine part, man.

Through her finer nature she is meant to keep her gaze directed upwards, for the drawing of those pure currents that are vital for the formation of what is pure and healthy here on earth and in the rest of the World of Matter. Her finer nature, which can also be seen in the generally finer and more delicate nature of her physical features, makes it so that the finer radiations can penetrate more readily and fully through her. She is therefore well-equipped to serve in the role of the receiver of primary power for the working of her species on earth and in matter. She is therefore the first to respond to that which is perceived as it comes down in the form of radiation to earth and its surroundings.

The masculine and positively active part of the species is to work more closely with the coarser substance of the earth, in a manner that does not require the fineness of the intuitive perception of the feminine, finer and negatively receiving woman. He is meant to put into more earthly and concrete form the volition that has been given a form by the more sensitive and receptive feminine part. He is meant to *execute* as the enforcer of this volition, the *workhorse* that makes it happen on earth as it has been received or perceived by woman. They *were* and *are* to work as equals in this effort, both abilities and qualities being absolutely necessary for the upbuilding work of spreading light on earth and in Creation.

Woman, however, is to stand a bit higher in the order of Creation for the purpose of receiving the necessary power currents, which then become available to the man only afterwards, and also more gradually, ...transformed. For this reason she is meant to keep her gaze directed upwards, the only way that she can make contact intuitively with that which comes from above and make it available through her being to her surroundings. A distraction from this can only lead to chaos and destruction, because it would mean a cessation in the flow of currents absolutely necessary for the formation of what lasts long and leads upwards.

Failure in this means the favouring and nourishing of works which, from their very beginnings, bear seeds of transience and destruction. They already start working their ways towards disintegration because they draw currents that lead to what is denser, overripe and in need of disintegration for the purpose of reformation into a more beautiful form, as is the case with everything material. What leads upwards draws spiritual currents, the energy that runs Creation, which keeps the forms vital, animated, fresh and away from overripeness; thus not-in-need of destruction through disintegration. It leads to eternal existence because it remains able to absorb and make *right* use of that which comes from Eternity. It is the capacity to make continuous use of that which comes from Eternity that makes the successful human spirit capable of existing in the Spiritual Realm, which is in the eternal Kingdom of God in Creation. There, there is no cycle that leads towards disintegration from seed, but an ever-freshness that is a mark of full consciousness.

Everyone can experience this happening if only he so wills and pays adequate attention, even in these times when mankind have sunken to very shameful depths. The idea that true power and strength lie in being able to perceive aright the nature of the working of the Laws of Creation, and to put this perception into practice for the good of everyone, is a difficult one to pass on to a mankind that has become so used to the physically visible expressions of power, which are truly only masculine in nature, and therefore quite limited and inferior, thus transient.

The latter cannot have the far-reaching and long-lasting effects of the finer working that is the woman's, due to the fact that it is not as penetrative in its nature, because it is denser, coarser and not as fine. The fineness of the woman's perceptive capacity makes her able to draw from heights that are not accessible to men of the same species. There, in that world or plane of perception, happenings would have taken on form already before that lower plane from which the coarser masculine can then draw intuitively. Here it is a question of the nature of the frequency of vibration perceived, which actually defines and demarcates worlds and planes of experiencing. That frequency which the woman has access to is inaccessible to the man. His is of a coarser and lower kind.

The frequency of movement determines the nature of the vibration of that which moves. The resultant vibration determines the kind of form that comes together due to similarity and harmony in resonance, as in an orchestra or a choir. So, one can say that the separations and groupings that occur naturally in nature, as well as within groups of people, are the result of the resonance or lack thereof that exists in the vibrations of the individuals or groups concerned, with regards to their relationships and interactions with one another. The higher the frequency, the higher the plane upon which the movement exists as an entity that can be experienced.

That which is finer is also at the same time of a higher frequency of movement. The fineness of the lighter, finer species allows it to move faster when placed under the same amount of pressure as a coarser, denser species of substance. In fact, the pressure is taken in differently as a consequence of the easier penetrability that belongs to that which is finer. So it is really more of a question of being able to feel and sense or perceive more, while residing on the same plane.

Woman occupies the position of the finer in comparison with man. How she makes use of this capacity is then quite another issue. When used aright this capacity permits her to reach those spheres of movement that the coarseness of man's perceptive ability cannot allow him to. She is therefore capable of drawing down those pictures that express the Will of the Light as they come down from above as radiations of light – light here meaning the radiance or the effect of the Being of the Light, Which is God. When she responds in the right manner to what she perceives, she simultaneously forms corresponding replicas of what has been perceived. What is formed in this manner can be called her volition, her innermost stirring and deepest desire. And she is always expressing this in response to the constant stream of radiations that she cannot avoid or hide from.

This, which has thus taken on form, goes on to have an influence on what impacts man, who then responds according to his own perceptive capacity, bringing the picture being perceived and transmitted by the human spirits in matter much closer to what is earthly and what is practical for life on earth. It is also the same in the other planes of matter.

In fact, it is the same throughout the entire Creation, right up to those heights which the human spirits developing in matter cannot attain to even in their most perfect forms.

As earth-woman is able to draw from a higher height, so she is able to have a greater sphere of influence and thus do more than any man can, if she uses her abilities rightly, i.e., if she strives steadfastly for what is good. It is similar to the situation where one on the twentieth floor of a tall building is able to see more of the surrounding area on the ground than one on the first floor of the same building.

The effects of the finer intuitive perceiving of the woman are also able to penetrate more deeply than those of man, and being spiritual, they have the capacity to attract and cause the attracted substance to move according to the volition that they express, which they bear at their core. So they can influence upwards everything in the World of Matter if they are as they should be, bringing about the upliftment of everything so touched due to its increased capacity (as a result of the upward-tending movement) to be attracted upwards by the higher spiritual beings above.

The more visible activity is the coarser one, which therefore makes it appear as the more powerful or influential one. But this is not so! It appears so to one with only a limited view of the whole. The form and the manner of use of the coarser capacity, as well as the consequent effect of its use, can only result from a prior formation or expression of volition by the finer feminine, whether it is a good one or not, and whether the feminine is conscious of this effect of hers or not. Whatever emerges from a particular people here on earth is a reflection of the nature of its womanhood, or of how the women of the people are regarded or looked upon by its men. What they express within, when they look at or think of their women, is what forms around them as their works, as what they have formed in response to what has been passed on to them by their women.

But that which is expressed by women does not remain restricted to the physical environment to which she is connected, but goes on to influence others in other parts of the world as well as ones who are no longer on earth, as long as the males so touched vibrate in a manner that allows for a connection with the vibration in question.

It is the same also with the smallest particles that are the first to form in the physical gross material earth. These are in constant motion, and this is an attribute of their fineness and sensitivity. Any impact at this level in the happenings on earth impacts the formation and consequent nature of that which eventually becomes visible. When the finer part is as it should be, or close enough to the perfection of the highest Heights, then only what is beautiful can come through the coarser and more positive-acting masculine, outer and more visible part, as a more visible expression of what has formed, and exist in a form that leads to more beauty, peace and harmony. It is similar to the manner in which the nature of the core of a fruit of a plant determines what eventually manifests on the outer part, and how enjoyable and beneficial this fruit will be to one who eventually eats it.

Today, it is misguided, this very visible masculine power (creative capacity), because the guiding feminine has for a long time been missing! The latter is needed in its rightful position in order for the true balance which alone can allow for the flow of true power to take shape. As has already been mentioned, the collaborative working of men and women in this venture does not require that the men and women even know of each other, but that they simply in their own lives give of what they have been blessed with, which can only be developed aright through striving upwards and drawing down those pure spiritual currents which are the energy currents that run Creation. Their natural abilities or talents will be pressed out in the forms of their intuitive perceptions, thoughts, speech and actions. Acting in this manner alone is the true worship of the One Who has made their existence and conscious experiencing of life at all possible – the Creator, God.

The experience associated with this happening, with the true worship of God, and which encourages its continuation or development, however, has rarely been had by men on earth. The actual experiencing of the working-out of the Laws of Creation, the Will of God, as it manifests in the life of the observing one, cannot but be seen as "magical" or miraculous; something that feels as though from "out of this world", and yet quite logical and real to him. Something that instills quite naturally the confidence and conviction in the existence of a lawful process through which everything and everyone is provided for, as long as he stands in the ray of light.

When woman voluntarily stands in the ray of light, i.e., when she makes the basis of her actions the desire to fulfill the Will of the Light, Which is expressed in the natural Laws of Creation, and not on vanity, the desire to be admired or noticed, or on fear, lust for earthly power and influence, or any of the other base reasons that often motivate people, then everything that forms around her as a consequence of this must reflect this volition, this deep intention, and must therefore take on a form that encourages her along that path. This means that the world around her will form more beautifully, because only such a development can lead to her being encouraged to continue along that path. What would stir in the species around her, including the masculine and executing part of her species – man, will lead to goodness and beauty, because that is what she would have sown with her finer intuitive perception. This is so, even if many a thing will have to be torn down first because it is wrong and cannot exist in the new time.

But she cannot fail to draw out from man and from everything else, as a natural consequence, what is ugly and oppressive, illogical and debasing, if through her inner activity she invites him (by attracting the volition for this from within him) to keep his gaze low and focused on the fulfillment of earthly desires as his primary goal. The quality of his work will reflect the wrongness of this focus. This, everyone who wishes to can see.

Briefly, here lies the mystery of the tempting of Eve with the forbidden fruit, and her passing on of the tasted fruit to her husband Adam, as is allegorically rendered in the Bible. The tasting of the fruit is the perception by woman of the dark volition that strives downwards towards the earth and away from the Light above. Such a perception has the effect of moving, and thus, animating something within the perceiver so that he vibrates to some degree in the same manner inwardly. If this is not checked, then the next natural step in that direction will follow and the taster will be led to where he can indulge even further in that which, through his inclination and expression of volition, he has declared his desire for.

Woman expressed this developing movement outwardly in several ways, including in the desire to be looked at and admired by the man. This was the beginning of vanity, which could then later on develop into various forms. Her gaze was low and directed at what was low, earthman and his attention. Man responded to what he tasted or perceived by doing those things that would make him more acceptable to the object of his desiring – woman. In his response he also admitted in the currents of vanity and gave it a form through his own nature. His desire to keep the woman and her attention drove him to strive more strongly for the accumulation of wealth and for earthly power and influence. This striving brought in its train all other evils. It kept his gaze lowered to the earth plane as a natural consequence.

As already mentioned, the basic animal or physical instincts for physical nourishment and enjoyment, as well as for procreation, due to their being one-sidedly animated through the over-developed intellect, developed into the beasts of lust (e.g. the dangerously over-developed sexual instinct) and avarice, which dominated and ruled over men. Nothing could be of greater importance to them over the course of millennia – during which they developed along their chosen course – than to satisfy as much as they could their ever-growing greed, vanity, distorted sensuality, conceit, the pursuit of and struggle for earthly power and influence, love of ease, spiritual indolence and ignorance. And everything in matter does develop!

In this way men transformed and multiplied the effects of the temptation that came through woman from Lucifer. One only needs to look at the perceived problems in the world today and he will identify one or more of the above-mentioned dark attributes at the core of the happening, as a driving force or motivating factor. They are all expressions of the one-sided focus on what is earthly, which naturally results in the stagnation and even retrogression of spiritual growth.

Such a narrow focus must always constrain the expansion of an energy-form such as the spirit in man. But it is the spirit alone which is able to draw the energy currents that bring and sustain life, for only the spirit is homogeneous in nature to these luminous currents! While living in spiritual poverty and ignorance, they could only produce works through their intuitive perceiving, their thoughts and actions, which led to chaos and destruction. This was inevitable because the fruit had to agree with the seed.

To disentangle themselves from the mesh of their own works would require that men acquire and apply the thorough knowledge of how the Laws of Creation work, and thus of how they (mankind) came to be so entangled. When the Son of God saw that the hold of these entanglements on men was very strong, owing to the degree to which they had sunken and could no longer produce and sustain lighter intuitive perceptions and thoughts, and that His Mission would be cut short because of this through the effects of what was developing in the ranks of the religious leaders who felt their influence on the people, and thus also their power, to be threatened by Him, He promised that Another would come at a later time Who would bring to them all what He (Jesus) could not tell them then. He urged them to trust in what He told them in His parables and teachings, and apply them in their daily lives in order to bring them alive within them. That was to keep them connected to the Source of all Power and on a path that would keep them from destruction in the time when reciprocal effects of their wrong seeds would return to them as blows, clearing the way for what adjusts itself to the natural Laws of Creation; the time of the *Final Judgement*.

What He therefore gave men was to sustain them and help them develop from that time until now; while they were on earth and also after they had left it for the necessary experiencing in the planes of matter beyond the earth that corresponded with the density of their souls. They were to come back to earth, if their necessary paths prescribed it, bearing the strengthened volition for what is good, thus increasing their chances of coming into contact with what the Helper would bring.

So, they were to maintain the right connection through their good volitions and actions, until the time when they could recognise and receive help from the promised Helper. He, the promised Helper, would then guide them with His Word through and around the obstacles that they had heaped along the paths that they individually had to travel back to their spiritual origin and to the Kingdom of God.

Discovery of what lay in the gift that Jesus brought to mankind with His teachings, and not what has been spread by men based on their limited and distorted understandings, could only be made through their steadfast application in the daily lives of men. Only in so doing could they gain that conviction that would permit them to *truly live,* i.e., with true bliss and happiness, even in the face of perceived obstacles and hardships, and thus anchor Jesus' teachings visibly on earth.

★　★　★

That Jesus had to travel around and speak to all who cared to listen meant that He could not make men *see* just by the wave of His hand. God does not work in such a manner. It would not accord with His own Will which always gives to a person the fruit of what he has sown with *his own* ability to decide. Jesus spoke to men so that in thinking over what He had said, which bore in it great Power because His words cloaked Divine currents (which have a much greater capacity to attract and control, and thus have more power than the spiritual currents), men could receive impressions upon their spirits which, through animating and attracting similar vibrations from deep within them, could allow their gaze to go upwards again; so that in the returning effects they could draw down *for themselves* those life-sustaining spiritual currents that power Creation.

In making their way outward through the *thoughts, words* and *actions* of men, these absorbed currents would also ennoble and beautify their surroundings, including the traditions and cultures of the various peoples of this earth, in strict accordance with what they would have willed for themselves as their gaze went upwards, in accordance with the working of the Divine Laws.

He came to help men make the right use of the energy currents in Creation for their own benefit, since spiritual death and natural extermination from Creation – the elimination of the formed spiritual personality – lay ahead for anyone who could not achieve this.

One should, if one were to look at the situation in this light, be able to see the tremendous sacrifice that lay in Jesus' coming to this part of Creation, where hostility was likely to confront Him as an Envoy of the Light, through those who had given themselves up for use for this purpose because they, like the majority of mankind at the time, no longer could recognise anything of the Light, having been so entangled in wrong conceptions and all varieties of human faults or weaknesses, which these false conceptions helped nourish.

Through men the Darkness ruled the earth at the time, and through them Jesus was confronted by it, and His earthly path was made as difficult and as torturous as it eventually became.

The pursuit of earthly power and influence, and the fear and distrust that go along with this one-sided striving, became the vehicle through which indescribable torture and premature physical death came to the Son of God; a Part of the Light sent down to help in re-directing the volition of men towards the Light, from Which alone they could draw the necessary helpful currents for their own salvation from entanglements, for their true enjoyment of life on earth, and for their rise, and thus, resurrection from matter! His murder was mankind's rejection of the Help. It was a decision that they made, since they had the freedom to exercise their freewill.

The treatment on earth of Jesus, Who was not guilty of anything, revealed the nature of the ethereal world surrounding the earth at the time of His incarnation on earth. What exists in the ethereal environment, in the world of volition and also of thoughts, which man cannot see with his physical eyes but which lives in the greater part of matter, shows itself in what manifests physically on earth, for earthly happenings are always an expression of what already has formed and exists in the finer Ethereal World of Matter. The revealed volition of men at the time when Jesus came to help mankind was one that sided with the Darkness and not with the Light. Through that dastardly and heinous act, men revealed how they stood inwardly with respect to their desire to *truly know* the Truth and abide by the governing Will of God.

Those through whom the torturous fate came to the Son of God represented earthly religion as well as government leadership, which goes to show the extent to which religion has not represented God, but only the volition of those who keep it going. This is so even if in the beginning it was formed to help men understand what had been brought by a messenger sent by the Light at some earlier time, and even if the intention still exists in many an adherent today to help spread word of the existence of God. That religion is something entirely by itself and completely separate from God and the true conception of Him, shows itself in the actions of many of those who call themselves believers today, and who, in the course of their daily lives, often feel compelled to go through the rituals that form the tenets of their particular religions. Through these men the tenets of the religions are opened up to everyone for examination.

The *reasoning* behind the doctrines to which they subscribe often stands very far from what can help a human spirit *recognise* and understand better the governing Laws of Creation, so that in *knowing* and abiding by them they may fulfill the Will of God and serve Him. By making their ways through the established rules and traditions of their religions, without at the same time troubling to see how these help *them* in the fulfillment of God's Will, they keep themselves from the paths that would naturally have led them *individually* to this knowledge.

Individual capacities of perception are not developed in such conditions because this is not encouraged, since every member must adhere to some common doctrines which identify him as a member of the particular religion. Moving away from this due to personal realizations and convictions becomes very difficult for many; it makes them outcastes from such religious groups. In trying to avoid this fate many disregard their inner perceptions and misgivings, and go against the Inner Voice as they unnaturally try to practice some rituals thought up or put into place by someone else.

If these rituals or doctrines helped someone or some people at some former time in coming closer to understanding the working of the Will of God, it does not mean that it would help another in the present time. Only that which has been perceived within, and which one has become convinced about through personal experience, can link him with those currents indispensible for the ascent and well-being of the human spirit. Only one who is able to draw down and make use of these currents can be called a servant of God, because he helps with the maintenance and further development of His Work, which is Creation.

The development and existence of conviction about the working of the Laws of Creation becomes impossible as long as man holds within him, as a *priority*, the upholding of the tenets of the religion to which he belongs. He places this over the volition to *know* the Will of God! But without this knowledge and its rigorous and steadfast application in everyday life, there cannot be any true happiness, peace or harmony for man and his surroundings. His path must lead in a direction that opposes the Will of the Light. He must stand in Creation as one who has not rightly developed his talents and thus, one who does not use them in the right way. He must therefore stand as one who steers the radiations coming to him in a direction that cannot be uplifting, no matter what his intentions might be. There cannot be any other possibility! His good intentions cannot make up for his lack of ability to make the right use of the power currents, just as little as the good intention of a three-year-old boy can empower him to safely drive a real car on a highway that requires the keenest attention from an experienced driver.

Where man is not able to rightly develop his talents then what abilities he has would be taken away from him, including the opportunity to exist as a conscious entity in Creation, because he would only be able to transmit what is negative to his surroundings. Just as was taught to man in one of the parables of Jesus.

Where there is not the conscious effort at striving to know and execute the Will of God here on earth, there also cannot be the perception and execution of this Will. The actions of the one involved, regardless of his intentions, must therefore be the opposite of this. It must, therefore, be made clear in the mind of the reader that the mention of God or of His Will in this work does not in any way refer to the practices or customs of religions that have existed until now, and which may persist for a little while longer in the future; or to the conceptions that have existed in the minds of many hitherto, but to the conceptions of God and His Will as They are expressed in the Laws of Creation which we can see everywhere.

Man is really only able to receive glimpses of the associated conceptions of God and His Will, but that which he is able to get for himself through an unrelenting *personal* effort will always enrich him and broaden his gaze; will bring him peace, happiness and true joy, and fill him with the confidence and courage to only move in the direction that supports this effort, as he is drawn upwards towards the Source of the animating and sustaining energy currents! It is this alone that is able to draw him back to his origin as one who has successfully completed the cycle of his development and is then able to serve the Light eternally, i.e., eternally draw and pass on those currents that come from the Eternal Power Source.

This requires that one becomes free from everything that keeps him from moving freely, which stifles his capacity to see beyond specific artificially set boundaries, such as comes through the rigid doctrines of established religions. The person concerned *must* act for himself, using his own perceptive and thinking faculties, using every ounce of strength that he can muster, because what he needs for his ascent can only come to him along a personal path of experiencing, never through some collectively agreed-upon concept that may not resound in his own intuitive perceiving.

All the teachings that were brought to men in the past regarding the Ways of God were to form steps in an upward development to the crowing Truth That man is now to receive. They were to prepare him for Its reception. Those messengers were Forerunners of the promised Spirit of Truth. The Message of the Spirit of Truth is identical to that of the Son of God, because they are of the same Origin – from within God Himself.

The Spirit of Truth is the Spirit of God, His Creative Spirit or Creative Will. Through Him Creation formed and remains sustained by the currents that He passes on from God to His Creation. It is this permanent position, as a bridge to Creation, that gave Him the name "the Son of Man", because He is that Son or Part of God Which stands closest to Man in His working. The Son of God came out of God, as a Part of His Love, to intervene in the downward spiral that mankind was caught in, for the sake of those who did not deserve destruction through disintegration, because the Love of God and His Justice cannot permit of such injustice. Such intervention was necessary to prevent the sealing of the fate of those who did not deserve it to a path that would irretrievably lead to destruction through disintegration.

In fact, the perfect Justice of God made it necessary that the Love of God intervene in such a manner. But the Love of God Who came down to us was not to stay with us in that form, because His Work of emergency intervention was done. It was not a permanent one, or one that was to keep recurring. He himself said that He would return to His Father after He left the earth following physical death. It is not necessary for the Love of God to remain in that form in Which It came, because the Will of God that sustains Creation cannot be separated from the Love of God, and so transmits the Love of God to man. He who perceives the Will of God in the right way also sees His Love at the same time. His Love is inseparable from His Justice and lies in everything that happens and could possibly happen. It is important that man understands this rightly, especially now when the Cosmic Clock thunders through the Universe and also on earth the *Hour of Twelve*.

Jesus promised to send Another to help mankind at a later date because that Other is more connected to Creation, being the eternal link to Creation from the Primordial Light – the Son of Man. He, the Spirit of Truth, Who is also referred to as the Holy Spirit because He is the Creative Spirit of God, is the Creative Will of God. It is His working or His Will that is seen in the Laws of Creation. It has been mentioned already above how the Will of God is borne by the natural Laws discernable to all. The working of the Creative Spirit is responsible for the beginning and conclusion of every cycle of development. Hence all cycles must begin and end in strict accordance with the Law of Development that reflects the Laws of Creation.

It is the cycle of radiations that begin and end with the Holy Spirit that formed and sustains Creation itself. For this reason He is the Alpha and Omega of Creation. The starting point of the radiations that come into Creation and the One Who receives the radiations that go upwards to the Light from the Creation. He is the Volition of God Which took on form as His Spirit for the purpose of Creating Creation. In Him works Almighty God as He creates.

As such, He also comes at the time when an epoch in the development of man on earth has come to an end and a necessary transition to a higher state is to be effected if everything, including the human spirits on earth and in matter, is not to be drawn down into the process of disintegration; a time that has to do with the closing of all cycles, for each individual human spirit as well as for the earth and the entire World of Matter as a whole.

It is the same with every single happening, whether minute in its significance or size, or great. It is the same with the beginning and end of every form that could be observed by man, such as the planets and the stars in the various solar systems, as well as atoms and all the molecules that could form from them, and the discovered and yet-to-be discovered subatomic particles. Their inceptions and ends follow the same logical process of coming together because of homogeneity, the production of fruit that corresponds with the homogeneity, and the falling apart due to over-ripeness in order for new and nobler forms to arise.

The process was and is the same for the development of the spirit of man on earth. In stages it received teachings about the nature of the working of the Laws of Nature which, as the Laws of God, form the support and the driving force for the formation and expansion of the entire Creation. It was to mature and grow from one state to another, just like a plant would. The expansion associated with its growth would have affected everything about the human spirit, including the conceptions held about God, the reason for the human spirit's being in the World of Matter and in Creation at all, and how it is meant carry to out its recognised responsibilities. The end of this process would have brought it to full control of its abilities and full lordship over its sphere of influence.

This lordship would, however, be nothing like the conceptions of lordship that generally exist in the minds of men today, but would be a consequence of a complete alignment of the perceiving, thinking, speaking and acting of man in ways that would agree with the Laws of Creation. For man to agree with these Laws in his actions would mean to act in just those ways as would draw to it spiritual currents from above, for he remains a spiritual being and can only be natural in a spiritual way of working.

This state of being would then naturally open up all that lies below the human spirit, including his material environment, to unblemished rays of light for the most beautiful and the noblest arrangements of material forms, in response to the attractive pull of even nobler forms in the higher spiritual spheres above; a pull which could then be effectively and purely transmitted through the ennobled human spirits.

To become able to do this man must first become thoroughly familiar with the nature of the working of the Laws of Creation and how this working manifests in the different planes of matter, including the earth-plane upon which he currently resides. The teachings brought at different intervals in the course of thousands of years were meant to help with the step-by-step progression upwards along this natural path. They were not supposed to form isolated parcels of belief systems, cut off from one another by the dissimilarities introduced through mankind's misinterpretations and wrong transmissions (due to narrow-mindedness, fear, distrust and another weaknesses), which keep them apart and enforce disharmony between the different associated groups. But they were supposed to help all mankind prepare for the time when they would have to make use of all their developed talents to participate in bringing this earth and matter into a paradise-like state, with the help of the One Who was promised mankind as the last Light-Bringer.

His recognition and the use of what He brings are indispensible for man's survival as a living entity, here on earth and also beyond earth-life. Man's ability to form an inner nature and an outer surrounding that would allow for continued passage of energy currents is dependent on his ability to know and adapt to the natural Laws of Creation.

Those who cannot do this remain bound to the limitations of their narrow perception, which is kept from growing because they delude themselves in most cases that they already know everything and need nothing new. They think that they already possess the key to the Kingdom of God through belonging to some religious group and through being able to recite and defend its tenets, as well as blindly carry out the associated rituals or traditions. They presume that mere outward gestures and displays of piety are enough to qualify them for entry into Paradise, their spiritual origin and home. They do not recognise and, therefore, cannot follow the weavings set off by their inner attitudes and intuitive perceptions (deep inner stirrings), from seed to fruit. They do not see what their conditions have to tell them about their inner attitudes. As a result they remain closed and conceited, narrow-minded and distrustful, and cannot in such a state admit rays from the Light into themselves for necessary growth and development; the adamantine and inexorable Law of Sowing and Reaping not allowing for it.

Their belief that their understanding of things is the right and final form keeps them from even *willing* or harbouring the desire to know more or better, hence nothing new comes to them, nothing penetrates to them, for it is their *own* volition for it that alone can allow for an approach, not to mention an entry into their souls, of what already exists in Creation, which could help them towards better and greater understanding. With any stagnation, however, upward movement ceases and decay or disintegration begins. It develops quite naturally towards its corresponding end.

Their assertion that the human spirit cannot know the *mysterious* ways of God is not born of *true humility* but is the mark of strong spiritual *indolence*; of a lack of spiritual movement, which in turn encourages *that* conceit that keeps men self-satisfied, and which causes them to fill in those gaps in their presumed knowledge with all kinds of false assumptions and impossible ideas about God and His Laws, so that the final picture that they and others form of Him cannot agree with logic, and is so badly distorted and dimmed that it completely prevents the perception of the Perfection, Love and Justice which cannot be apart from God or His image.

They keep away from the true knowledge of God and His Will through this, because they do not humbly take in what comes to them for consideration, even though it could not have come to them along their own personal paths by accident or for no reason. For, something within them must have drawn it to them reciprocally and, therefore, as a necessary experience *for them*.

The ways of the Creator must agree with logic, for the Laws of Creation or the Laws of Nature are *Logic* themselves; the strictest and purest forms of it, perceptible to some degree in their perfection only by that person who endeavours to test them out for himself through earnest and dispassionate observation of himself and his surroundings. Only then can he get glimpses of the true nature of the working of the Laws of God in Creation. It is therefore the case that all that men have thought of God until this time, i.e., the picture that they have held of the nature of the working of His Will in Creation, has been a very badly distorted and wrong one, especially when one considers the degree to which man has been equipped to perceive and, therefore, to truly *know*.

It is only because of this wrong picture or conception that men have come to expect unnatural happenings from the One Whose Will Itself is expressed in the Laws of Nature, in the *natural* Laws. Moving forward with this false picture and wrong expectations, men have further closed themselves to what will lead them to the Truth.

Many expect that He will bring them good fortune when they have asked for the opposite through the way they have attuned themselves within and therefore conducted themselves, beginning with their deepest inner feelings and manifesting in the outermost expressions of these feelings in physical deeds. By not drawing the straight line between cause and effect they never get to see the strict logic that lies in the Law of Reciprocal Action as it brings them their fates.

The narrow and superficial ways in which many view happenings around them also show themselves in the confinement of their perceptions to this earth and to this one earth-life, not allowing for the thought to be entertained within them of a much wider world where the same Laws work uniformly but in different forms, or of the possibility of other earth-lives prior to their current ones, during which time they also sowed seeds, as spiritual beings, which contributed to the world and environment that have formed for them according to their volition, and which they *must* therefore live through also in their current earth-lives in order to experience what they have consciously or unconsciously willed; the only way that they can bring the cycles of such deeds to a close and thus redeem them and themselves. Such occasions also offer them opportunities to become knowledgeable of the true effects of their inner attitudes and outward deeds so that they can work more consciously going forward and avoid further entanglements which will demand further acts atonement from them.

What was sown in past earth-lives, but which has not yet been atoned for and redeemed, and so, which is still clinging to men as it continues to develop and grow, brings forth fruits that become interwoven with those of the fresh seeds sown in their current earth-life. The combinations bring about different effects, enhancements of what was already developing and coming to man, or a diminishment of it due to the difference between the old and the new. Thus an evil volition can enhance existing evil volitions to lead to enhanced effects, and a good one can diminish the effects of a prior evil one.

Without the closing of the cycle of the seed sown, and without the right recognition of the seed in the matured fruit, as well as the right adjustment of the one concerned to the Will of the Light following this recognition, he must remain bound and unable to ascend. He cannot then escape from the realm to which he is bound when the time comes for that realm to undergo its natural process of disintegration. He will have to partake of this process, being linked to it through his self-willed attachment to what has to disintegrate.

This agrees with his desire to be linked to that which is subject to the process of disintegration, even if this *desire* is not spoken of or thought of by the one concerned in a manner that oversees the range of consequences connected with the decision. But the inability to see the kind of end to which this desiring leads is the fault of the one concerned, because several attempts have been made by the Light to bring this to the attention of men, who, without any extra help, were already equipped with the capacity to perceive the simplicity associated with the working of the natural Laws.

What is material and subject to disintegration and reformation, therefore, subject to change and transformation, includes the conceptions that we hold regarding the Creator and His Will. Where these do not develop upwards, as they must if we wish for clarity, harmony, peace and joy, as creatures of His Creation, then they would not be allowed to exist further when the earth or the material plane in question has to be raised upwards in its natural upward development. That which cannot keep up with the new vibration because it is of a lower kind, will undergo disintegration simply due to the lack of homogeneity that would exist between the new and the old vibrations. It simply would not be part of that which would make up the new and nobler formation, in the natural process of reformation following disintegration of the old in the upward development of all matter. The conceptions must therefore change in an upward manner or else rigidity will ensue, keeping it locked-in in a particular form, and forcing into being the derailment of the person who remains so bound through it.

Those who remain connected with the disintegrating conceptions and forms will experience the process in a form that corresponds to the human species. The painful effects of this process would be connected to those points in the lives of the ones concerned where wrong conceptions are alive and striving. This will, if they are fortunate enough to see, bring to their awareness the wrongness and hollowness of such conceptions, bringing them to the point where they could express the genuine desire for what is new and better, and what would aid them in their adjustment to the new time and vibration.

The pain and despair associated with being torn away from the disintegrating wrong conceptions and ideas brings to the fore the need to re-address those conceptions, to question the reasons for their adoptions by us, and to see if their foundations are indeed sound enough or in need of reconstruction. The newly constructed foundations and structures would only stand in the new time if they vibrate aright and not against the rhythm of the workings of the Laws of Creation. This will require knowledge, and knowledge can only come through personal experience.

Those who wish to serve God must come to know this because the knowledge of it lies along the path which they *must* tread individually if they are to successfully do so; for to *truly* serve Him is to do His Will in every aspect of life, on earth and also beyond earth-life. It is in the course of the uplifting discoveries made along this personal path of experiencing, with all the exertion that this will entail, that the talents of the particular individual concerned is developed, for it is only truly and fully developed when the direction of his gaze is upwards.

This is because, like everything else, the upward development of such talents requires that they be drawn upwards by a force which already stands higher. It is this which brings about growth; volition directed towards something higher. It is only in this direction of movement that the talents can make contact with the nourishing currents from above for their right formation and development. What is expressed inwardly and outwardly by one so involved cannot be shared or duplicated by others in its exact form, for it is unique to that particular individual. In discovering and making use of this in the right way, he contributes to the perfection of his species and thereby serves his Maker. He becomes a transmitter of light, a useful creature in Creation. For this reason he must personally experience this process. There is no other way to it. He must be determined to move within himself unceasingly.

This service happens in the moments of the hours of the days of the life of the person concerned. What man bases his every decision on, that is, every movement or stirring within him in response to a flashing thought or in preparation for an inner or an outer movement, determines how that particular movement develops, i.e., in which direction it strives. In the same way as what develops to become visible and tangible to man on earth first *physically* manifests in the realm of subatomic and atomic substances, which are constantly vibrating under the pressure of the prevailing spiritual volition of their surroundings, what develops for man as his fate starts at the level of the moment, the very present, the basic unit of time during which a seed is sown and the future tapestry of the fate of the sower is changed. This agrees with the saying: "small causes, great effects".

It is in the present that the decision is made, that the vibration leaves man according to how he feels upon receiving some impulse from within or from outside of him. This released energy-form already starts to go along its elliptical cycle of development, during the course of which it attracts or is attracted by other similar forms, depending on its strength, in order to return to the originator as developed fruit, as a part of his psychic and physical condition, thereupon causing him to respond again according to how he stands at the time of the return of the matured fruit.

During this time, activities in the finer worlds of matter, which are connected to their originator residing on earth, lead to similar happenings or developments in the coarser worlds, right down to the earthly environment that man is able to physically feel and touch. What develops for him here therefore depends on what has formed for him in the finer planes through which the animating light rays that move Creation must first pass, in moving *from above downwards,* in accordance with the formation of Creation, which always has finer and lighter substances standing higher and preceding denser ones.

In the passage of the energy currents from above downwards, the finer substances of matter are moved accordingly and man is compelled to respond to how this movement strikes him, because he bears within himself, as inner cloaks around his spirit, the substances of all the planes of matter. His inner response determines what develops and forms for him in those planes that correspond to the finer material cloaks that envelop his spirit as parts of his soul. That which he forms sinks or rises, depending on its weight and density, linking him more firmly with what is light or what is dark. What he has formed with the finer substances of matter influence the formations for him in the denser and coarser planes of matter. In this way he continually forms a world that is his alone, that is *built* from his own point of view, and that admits of only what is homogeneous to this, keeping everything else out as a natural process.

The fineness of the lighter substance makes it able to penetrate the denser, coarser one, in the same way as certain rays of fine substances here on earth (such as gamma rays or wireless communication rays) are able to penetrate solid substances. What therefore is expressed in the moments of decision-making, which are in most cases lived through un-consciously or without adequate consciousness by man, forms a thread that is woven in as a part of the fabric that represents the fate that he has to live through in his future, on earth and also in the beyond after earth-life.

As human spirits with the capacity to form volition, which has attractive capacities of various strengths, that which permeates what is coarser and denser also exerts something like a magnetic pressure upon it, thus forming it according to its own nature.

In this way, as has already been mentioned above, many homogeneous or similar threads come together as homogeneous fruits, which shape and define the psychic and physical conditions in a person's life, with each fruit dovetailing in with other homogeneous fruits, so that there is a natural flow from one to the other, and a natural working -together towards a collective, homogeneous goal.

The end-result of this development through combinations of similar forms, originating from similar volitions or desires, can only be changed for better or for worse through changing the nature of the seed sown in the moment. In this way man strives upwards to the Light or he sinks downwards to the regions ruled by the Darkness, the strength of which is contributed to by the base or dark works of men. There, in the dark regions, ignorance and non-adherence to the Laws of Creation thrive and are expressed in varied forms by the resident human spirits, so that only distorted and ugly works that bring pain and lead to destruction can be found.

I pointed out in the beginning of this book that the nature of what is formed gives evidence of the kind of energy (or energy forms) that led to its formation. The pure spiritual currents that are available for use by men can only form what is good and what leads upwards to unimaginable states and planes of existence, where joyous activity, which only strengthens, brightens and ennobles, reigns. Through attracting and becoming individually cloaked in denser and denser substances, through the nature of our increasingly denser and narrower conceptions, we made ourselves only able to access energy currents which consist of heavily laden particles, at the cores of which naturally were very weak spiritual sparks, which did not receive the impetus towards greater frequency of movement and the consequent formation of more beautiful forms; the impetus which was to be transmitted by maturing human spirits that were to become aglow in the course of their own upward movement in matter. The human spirits had failed to mature.

Such densely-coated particles, which formed the currents that alone we had access to, through being homogeneous to them because of our own heaviness, could only form combinations that led to environments that accorded, in their ugliness and ponderousness, with our inner natures. Man's self-subjugation to the earth-bound intellect placed a boundary on the extent of his perception and thus on the nature of the currents that he was able to draw. The lower vibrations of these impure currents could only lead to certain corresponding combinations, the end-products of which could also only transmit what was distorted and far from the brilliance of the logical working of the perfect Laws of Creation. Hence, the adverse and often horrible conditions that have prevailed on earth in the course of several millennia.

We have in the past and are currently experiencing such distortions in the course of our earth-lives. When help was sent to us, we viewed the bringers and what they brought through the same veil of distortion and dimness, thus changing its meaning and moving the points of emphasis to suit the existing distortion and the human faults and weaknesses that go with it. Rigid religious doctrines were formed which did not lead men to a better understanding of the nature of the working of the Will of God on earth, and so men never truly learned the true purpose of their existence on earth, and also were not moved through the naturally-accompanying personal experiences to truly change the nature of their inner activity and thus produce better forms.

In order to help those who wished for it overcome the self-inflicted impediment to being able to see clearly and act rightly, so that everpurer currents (thus, currents of spiritual particles that are less and less coated with material substances, which, as alien substances, act as impurities) would flow through them to their surroundings, and so that the combinations thereof would bring about only wonderful conditions, Jesus promised those listening and willing to receive that help to ask His Father to send Another, following His (Jesus')departure from the earth, Who will remind men of what He (Jesus) had said (because He would come from the same Source or Origin), and Who would lead them to the knowledge of the Truth.

He called this *Other* the Spirit of Truth, and He has also been referred to as the World Teacher, because He will teach willing listeners to know the World as it is, how it works and how to live in it aright. He would bring to conclusion the work begun by Jesus when He came two thousand years ago, bringing emergency help to those who did not deserve to suffer disintegration with the rest of mankind, which latter had bound themselves to the malformed and disintegrating material world through subjugating themselves to the earthbound intellect, while simultaneously cutting themselves off from the Spiritual Realm.

The World that men could know through the World Teacher encompasses much more than what men could ever hope to examine using physical tools presently available to them or yet to be invented, because physical tools can only interact and deal with what is physical. But the greater World, within which the same Laws of Creation work as a *governing Principle*, comprises realms the substances of which are different from that of the physical environment of the earth, making them undetectable or unobservable using physical means. It can only be perceived intuitively by the spirit, which is within us as the animating and only living part of us; which is indeed the real man. It is this part which has the capacity and the task to weigh and examine, and then to express the resultant impression outwardly through the physical body, which is controlled through the brain.

It is necessary now for man to understand the entire process connected with his existence and his activity on earth and in the material world in general, for only in so doing can he make the right use of what tools he has for directing aright the energy currents coursing through Creation and also through him. Anything short of the complete understanding of the truth of these happenings would leave a gap through which man would fall to his spiritual death – the end of the possibility of his being able to transmit anything as a personality in Creation; because this personality would have been destroyed after having proved, over the course of the time allotted to it for its development, to be incapable of participating in the upbuilding work in Creation that is willed by God. He would have chosen to bind himself to what is transient and subject to disintegration, and he would have determined his fate thereby.

With the teaching of the World Teacher, mankind can understand the fruits that come their way every moment, recognise the seeds that led to these fruits, and become able to sow only the kinds that will bring about, in the perfection of the Laws of Creation (the Law of Reciprocal Action, the Law of Attraction of Homogeneous Species and the Law of Gravity), conditions that will aid in the growth and sustained nourishment of the Volition: Let There be Light. For, with His coming He brings to life on earth a corresponding form of the Holy animating Will: Let There Be Light!

The Coming of the Other, Who is the World Teacher, must naturally be accompanied by a great influx of energy currents such as the world has never experienced before. This is because His Origin, Which is in God Himself, as is that of Jesus, goes together with a capacity for attraction and movement that the purest and highest of spirits cannot come close to imagining.

His Coming naturally happens in the world that is natural for men. By this I mean that along their individual paths of experiencing men will encounter the effects of this happening. It would not be something that lies outside of the logic of natural development. So the process of development would be discernable by men if they look with the right tools; intuitive perception for that which is spiritual and higher than what is earthly, and the rightly-guided intellect for that which is detectable with the physical senses.

The One Who comes brings help to man on earth in a form that he is able to see and feel, which is tangible to him and thus easily recognizable if he wishes for it, and which gives evidence of the Helper's prior cognition of the world of men.

In other words, the expected One comes as a man among men, armed with the experiences acquired while living as a man on earth, outwardly a man but with a Core that comes from the Light; the only natural way that an Envoy of the Light can make physical contact and interact tangibly with mankind. To seek Him in what is unnatural, as many have done in trying to understand Jesus and His Father, will be to miss Him!

Jesus already warned against this in the parable of the Ten Virgins, which He gave to emphasize for men the importance of keeping alert through striving for what is good and light, because only that will link them to the path along which they will come upon and recognise the One Who bears Light on earth, and Who alone could lead them out of their self-imposed entanglements upwards to the Light. This happening, for those concerned, shall not be limited to, nor shall it require the personal meeting of the One from the Light, but shall involve coming into contact with His Work, here on earth or after departure from it, and benefiting from it for their spiritual ascent.

In the parable given to mankind by Jesus, five of the ten virgins waiting for the Bridegroom did not prepare themselves by having adequate oil or fuel for their lanterns. When they ran out of fuel and had to go out to find some more, they missed the Bridegroom who arrived in their absence and whom they were all waiting for, and for the sighting of whom they had the lanterns in the first place.

One who wishes to recognize and thus benefit from the Coming of the Helper must therefore prepare himself through becoming able to see more simply, more naturally, and to harbor deep within him the earnest desire to serve the Light through abiding by Its Will. He has to prepare himself from within in order to *see* the effects of the Coming of the Helper, Whose ways can only be homogeneous with what serves the Light. It is his volition to do this that will form for him the path here on earth and beyond towards receiving of what the Helper has to offer. Only then could he be in a position to receive and make use of it.

The right volition or inner attitude is represented by the fuel needed for the lantern in the parable. The lantern, which as a tool needed for clearer vision and perception, represents the perceptive capacity needed for right cognition by the one concerned.

That person who desires to be persuaded, chased after or pleaded with, just so he can get what benefits him, and who therefore lacks the earnest volition to receive what the Helper brings with Him, will miss everything that could have helped him rise out of the state in which he has placed himself through his own volition. He will not see what he has not prepared himself to see; a preparation that can only occur through a change in his inner attitude, and which *must* become manifest in a new way of thinking and acting.

He cannot be convinced without making the effort towards this conviction himself, because conviction comes from personal experience, which requires the earnest testing and examining of all that is given as help. He shall wait with an arrogant and conceited attitude until he has run out of time to make the necessary changes to his nature, and then has to confront the forces that, in bringing him the fruits of his *true* desires, will overwhelm him due to his incapacity.

His lack of preparation and readiness, due to the faults which he has harboured and nourished within him, would become expressed in his being dragged very quickly in the opposite direction from that in which the helping hand of the Lord would have taken him. Along this path he would find those who would make it even more difficult for him to want to investigate that which is brought to help him. He shall find homogeneous souls.

The excruciating pain associated with the experience would be even more wholly felt because the coverings around his spiritual core, which have kept it bound for ages, would also be torn apart during this time, since they would also go through the *quickened* process of disintegration as forms that are old and useless for the necessary upbuilding, thereby leaving it open to the glare of the uncompromising Light, and making him see immediately, as if in a flash, all that he has missed with the way in which he has made use of the time of development allotted him in the World of Matter. A time which now comes to an end for him with his realizing that he has just missed the final opportunity for a turnaround and cannot in any way regain this opportunity.

He realizes that he cannot roll back the process of the increasing separation between what can be allowed to develop and grow stronger, and what must be destroyed if there is to be peace and harmony in the World of Matter and in Creation. The tearing off from him of that which is material and alien to his spiritual core will be experienced by him as very painful psychic and physical conditions; in other words, it would not happen in a gradual and soothing way. The time to prepare for a gradual separation has already passed.

The Coming of the Helper also brings about a change in the Volition that *leads* here on earth and in the entire Creation, because the associated Power of Attraction of the One Who comes cannot but bring everything in His surroundings into the mould of His Own Will. This occurs through the natural process of the stronger magnetically having a hold on all that is weaker. This marks an end to the reign on earth of the volition of the human spirit, since the human spirit can no longer be the strongest entity, producing the forms with the strongest collective magnetic effect on everything else.

Today, we are experiencing the rapid closure of all open cycles. It appears as though no sooner has one expressed a volition, be it in his thoughts or with his words or physical actions, than the consequences return to him fully laden with reciprocal effects, good or bad. We are experiencing a quickening of all cycles of development. Things that would have taken years to mature and bear fruit are developing to the point of harvest in minutes. All activities are as if in a state of heightened animation. There clearly is an influx of a great amount of energy.

Everything is now being forced to form differently, according to a different mould, determined by the Will or Nature of Him Who is from the Light. The same Law that caused everything on earth to form in accordance with the darkened inner nature of mankind, over the course of several millennia, now brings about the rapid *collapse and reformation* of everything according to that which is stronger and purer; a transformation to a world under a new Leadership, under the influence of a different Force Field. This transformation, however, would not feel pleasant to all, only to those who align themselves in time with what is good and upbuilding in nature; neither will it come in a gradual and mild manner, but will come with the suddenness, aggressiveness and severity that expresses the extent to which mankind have strayed from the Will of the Light, and the sharpness of the difference between what has been and what *should* be. Only he who serves the Will of the Light today by adjusting himself to the Laws of Creation can experience this period peacefully and joyfully.

The forms that will have to come together as a consequence of this influx of power cannot but express the vitality that is inherent in the purity and nature of said currents. The purest form of the animating energy currents must also have the greatest capacity to animate. It is due to the purity of the currents that they come with an intensification of power-pressure (increased magnetic capacity, which draws upwards to the Source of these pure currents), so that all developments are greatly quickened in their cycles. The greater purity and higher origin of said currents must lead to greater capacity of movement, thus more power. All cycles, without exception, must develop faster to their ends, either towards disintegration or towards upliftment and ascent.

What was already developing as the fruit of man's works (whether good or bad) will very quickly ripen and return to him for reaping under this immense Light-pressure. What might have in the past come back to a person for reaping in a future earth-life now comes to him in the present one. Mankind would now be faced with all that they have caused to come into being but which has not yet been severed from them, from past lifetimes on earth as well as from their present ones.

The encased spirit particles that animate the material world as energy currents, and which are implicated in the forms that have been created by men, in seeking to move towards this great Source of Power, under its immense attractive influence, are now vibrating faster and driving said forms quickly to their ends so that, in discharging the fruits of said developments to their originators, they can be released and freed up. In this happening, the beings that put into form for man everything that he intuitively perceives, thinks and does, form the bridge between man and what develops for him, because it is they, these beings, who fashion for man exactly that which he has willed, in strict accordance with the Law of Sowing and Reaping, the Law of God, since they exist and live to fulfill this Will in all of Creation.

Many of the fruits are coming to man in explosive forms due to the not-gradual nature of this sped-up discharge. It is indeed as though this discharge is being done under immense pressure. Hence the explosive nature of the goings-on today between individuals, couples, peoples, nations, races, classes and so on.

Since in all of this man only gets what is rightly due to him, nothing more and nothing less, exactly as he desired it through the way he laid the foundation for his thinking, speaking and acting, what he gets back in this time is therefore an expression of the assessment of his inward standing, of what he has yet to make good and what he has to enjoy, according to the seeds that he sowed with his capacity to generate forms using the creative power of the Will of God. It is Judgement as it has been designed by him who must now reap, through the decisions he has made and which had not until the present born fruit.

It is the *Final Judgement* because the intensity of the developments send the different species of forms very quickly to their homogeneous groups, whether light or dark, so that the gap between light and darkness is greatly increased, making it impossible for there to be a bridge in existence for the crossing over from one world to the other.

The increased pressure brought about by the quick ripening of all previously sown but as yet not-harvested fruits for each person, places him as though at the end of a powerful laser beam, which has the effect of cracking all that has calcified over and around his spiritual core, so that it *may* experience the flash of Light and be quickly drawn to an expanded state through increased activity. That spirit which does not take advantage of the happening for his ascent shall also be quickly swept along to that part of Creation where it has expressed a desire for, and where all that is old and *useless* must undergo destruction through disintegration. It shall be repelled with just as much force as it could have been attracted upwards with, had it made itself correspondingly more homogeneous to the Judging Ray.

The cracking of that which covers the spirit is the effect of the quickening of all developments, due to the increase in power currents brought about by the activity of the Envoy from the Light. In a relatively short period of time, men would have to experience quite a lot in their lives because the fruits of the seeds of their far and recent pasts would be brought to them for their experiencing as though all of a sudden, compressed into a short span of time, in the fulfillment of the Law of Reciprocal Action.

They shall know themselves through this, because they shall see how they stand through what comes to them for reaping, and what response the intensified pressure draws out of them. It is in this way that they shall be judged by and through their works. If these accumulated fruits are distasteful the pressure would bring intense pain. It would bring miraculous happenings if they are good fruits, encouraging the recipients to continue along those paths that allow them to know more of and to heed the Laws of Creation.

But whatever their nature, these fruits shall present the ones concerned with the opportunities to experience the perfect working of the Laws of Creation, which are also known as the Laws of Nature, and which are manifestations of the Will of God. Mankind should endeavour to go through the associated conditions with a sincere feeling of gratitude for the grace offered through such opportunities to *know* and to adjust their inner lives accordingly.

The right understanding and appreciation for the reason for our being allowed to live on earth, which is today being brought to the attention of men, would help earthman with the fostering of a sincere sense of gratitude, which, in being so different from the usual conceited frame of mind of the "modern man", can allow for clearer perceptions and better inward adjustments. Man would now have to thoroughly know Creation and all the Laws operating in it in order to have that inner capacity to recognise the help inherent in the happenings of the present time, and express gratitude for them.

A separation would be achieved quite naturally through the dissimilarity that would exist between people, due to the decisions they would have made under the immense pressure of the animating Light. This is a taste of the effect of the extraordinary and humanly unimaginable animating capacity held within the Primordial Light, God, the Source or Origin of Life and thus of all movement in Creation.

When a Part of the Primordial Light comes to the World of Matter and to earth, everything is greatly sped up as a natural consequence, because the energy that drives every happening in the first place comes from the Primordial Light, and a Part of the Primordial Light bears this capacity within Itself and naturally radiates Its effects in a corresponding way to the environment that It is in.

As has already been mentioned several times, the closeness in nature of a human being to the Primordial Light (to the extent that this is possible for the human being) leads to his (the human being's) increased transmission of this animating energy current and thus to the quick drawing together of material substances for the quick development of beneficial and uplifting forms. The power drawn from the Light in the form of spiritual currents increases the *creative urge* within the recipient. With the receipt or absorption of this increased urge the one concerned is moved to give fresher and newer expressions of the workings of the perfect Laws of God, which express His Will.

Fresher and newer expressions only come to him who strives towards the Origin of the creative urge. They are evidence of the absorption of power from the Light. This power flows eternally and can be eternally absorbed by the human spirit that has shown itself to be capable of absorbing and making use of it aright. The part that he plays in the growth that results from this is the contribution which the spirit makes towards the expansion of Creation. With the Will of the Light in the lead for the first time in this part of Creation, the only kind of growth that shall be sustained is that which accords with this Will.

This entails upward development, because it leads to the expansion of the world or realm in which Light reigns. Only one who gains knowledge of this Will through personal experience can inwardly move in such a way as produces the effects which can be called upbuilding works, that is, which can be said to be in line with the Will of the Light. Existing only to reproduce in other forms that which others have already drawn down through their own efforts, is an expression of spiritual indolence and incapacity; a contraction of the spirit due to a lack of energy-flow, a lack of connection to the stream of spiritual currents that always bear within them *fresh urgings* towards creativity and expansion. It is a sign of death, absence of life and lack of movement.

The effect of the ongoing purification in the Judgement is the separation of the *living* from the *dead*. The dead would naturally go together with that which has no life of its own and which is transient in nature – the material substance of the material world. For this reason the dead will experience the disintegration of the spiritual personality which they have formed in the several millennia during which human spirits have been developing in matter.

The *living* will naturally and steadily rise into that world that does not go through disintegration, because the substances of said world bear mobility within them, and as a result can be said to be alive. It is the substance of this world that transmits the effects of Life proper, God, to that which is transient and without its own warmth and mobility. This world, which has its own warmth and mobility, is the Spiritual World from which the human spirit in matter descended as seed. There, in the Spiritual World or Plane, the mature human spirit needs fear death through disintegration no more. He is at home and has proved to be capable of making the right use of the Power that comes from God for the right purpose in Creation. It is his ability to do this that makes it at all possible for him to enter and maintain himself there.

He who is content with reproducing the old, and who does not trouble himself to discover why he is in existence in Creation, places himself amongst the old and the useless, because fresh formations and expansion cannot happen through such a person. If pure spiritual currents bear urgings towards creativity and expansion, and if the spiritual currents need to be made use of in order for them to continue to flow, i.e., to have the reason to continue to flow to and through this part of Creation, then it follows that one who is not capable of developing and making use of his own unique talents for this purpose cannot survive the purifying flames, which come with the Divine Activity of the Envoy from the Light. The Flames come to rid the earth of all that is dead and incapable of transmitting light.

The purifying flames act like the antibodies and other disease-fighting cells in the human body, which eliminate cells infected by invading and potentially dangerous viruses and other pathogens. In the same ways as men would view such elimination as good and right, so would they become able to see the Justice and the Love that lie in the inability of human spirits that do not rightly develop their God-willed talents to exist amongst others who choose to, and who therefore do. What comes through those who cannot do this would continue to cause harm, chaos and disease, in the various ways that these manifest. There would continue to be a multiplication of what is evil and wrong, to the detriment of the surroundings of those concerned and all those within such surroundings.

Man needs to develop his unique talents for the purpose of transmitting the power currents in Creation in a manner that is fresh and useful. Anything else would mean a duplication, which is not needed in the necessary upbuilding in Creation. And since he who tries to imitate cannot be like the original and must be different in some way from the original, duplication is, from the beginning, impossible. Such a person becomes someone who is quite unstable, being neither this nor that. There can never develop the necessary trust and conviction needed for the execution of the Will of the Light in such a state.

Therefore, man must develop his inherent talents in order to be a useful creature. He must be able to absorb the creative urgings, the creative power, the energy currents in Creation, pure spiritual currents. This alone can press out his true talents in their most beneficial and only useful form. To strive towards this must be the goal of any person who wishes to remain useful. It is the highest goal that can be attained by a human spirit.

What is also quickened in this process is the transformation from the old to the new of the one concerned, in terms of conceptions and understanding of the workings of the Laws of Creation. It also means that what will come to this person along this noble path must be beautiful and pleasant, as soon as he has removed from himself the layers of alien dross covering his spirit. The beauty and pleasantness of the experience for this person will correspond to the degree of purity of the currents that will flow to him as a consequence of his upwardly-directed volition.

Such a person, as is described above, is able to experience life on earth as a Paradise, even in the midst of chaos, because what he forms for himself in all the turmoil would always come together in a way that will bring him joy, and leave him even more confident that a good seed always leads to what is good, while a bad seed cannot fail to diminish what is light. He will also see that what is light and what is dark or base always show themselves correspondingly in the way they manifest and are experienced on earth.

So, the apparent chaos around him, which is due to the breakdown everywhere of everything that has not been formed with the volition to know and serve the Will of the Light, will only serve to strengthen his confidence in the perfect working of the Laws of Creation. He will know in the midst of it all that he only needs to stand aright, steadfastly, with clarity and courage, in the midst of the happening, in order to always get what he needs and feel the protection that comes through being in line with the nature of God, as far as this can be humanly achieved.

That which comes into rhythm with this nature cannot be in need of dissolution for the purpose of reformation. It is as it should be and can avoid the pain associated with the tearing apart that occurs during disintegration. In always developing upwards it will continue to change for a better form, through humbly opening itself to the help which can only come from above, so that it always maintains itself above that plane or level where disintegration, with its attendant experiences, has to take place.

Matter must go through the process of disintegration at a certain point in the cycle of its development, because it is not able to rise to the level of perfection where disintegration for the purpose of reformation in a better state is no longer necessary. But the human spirit, in its perfected form, that is, back in its origin in the Spiritual Realm, does not need to concern itself with disintegration, because it does not take place there. He must therefore strive to perfect himself beginning here on earth, or else he cannot be attracted upwards to that plane where perfected spirits reside.

To do this he must be able to respond rightly to the goings on around him in order not to be drawn into the cycle of events that lead to disintegration. He must have attained to a thorough knowledge of the Laws of Creation in order to know how to navigate through the maze that has been formed through mankind's ignorance over several millennia, and which is now collapsing onto itself due to the rottenness and hollowness within its walls and its foundation. He needs help for this because he is no longer able to see clearly his way out of the self-created chaos on his own. Only One Who can have a view of the entire happening, from the very beginning to the end – an end which lies in the future of the successful human spirit – can provide man with a guide, a map of some sort, to help him make his way out of the collapsing maze, which is as though on fire and filled with smoke, as well as with the other fallout effects of a quick rise to bloom that is followed quickly by a collapse or burst.

The help that can get man out of this chaos must come from above, through the canopy of false conceptions that his narrow view has erected and continues to support. Man must be able to recognise and seize this help, with everything that he has, every ounce of strength that he can muster, in order to be able to make his way upwards through the blockades that lie above him, which he put in place on every step on his way downwards.

The help must be able to teach him about Creation and the Laws that govern it, in a manner that leaves no gaps.

Only with such help will he be able to walk the *personal* path that he *must,* in a manner that leads him through the liberation from his entanglements in matter, and upwards to his spiritual home. When this help is made use of in the right way, it will bring about a transformation within the person concerned, just as the world around him would have gone through a transformation – a quick process of disintegration of what is old (such as is going on now) alongside the development of what is new through those who have absorbed the help. Only such people would be able to exist in a world that has been transformed into a new state, such as would be in existence at the end of this on-going purification process, and one in which the Will of the Light alone rules.

Today, as has also be prophesied, many false prophets abound, promising all manner of things to vulnerable dupes who, in suffering from the consequences of their past mistakes and misdirection of energies, are crying out in apparent need of help. Many succumb to the enticements of the false prophets because these only play on their weaknesses, their craving for earthly power and influence, their love of comfort and ease, their vanity and conceit, their greed and selfishness, and their lust for earthly pleasures and gain.

Everyone can see the effects of these people and their works. These effects are also part of what men have asked for with their well-developed spiritual sluggishness. The collapse of the works of these trusted ones, who like to call themselves materialists and intellectuals, quite apart from those within the various religious groups who claim to know the way to the Light and can act in the place of God in the dispensation of Justice and Reward, can be seen all over the earth today. These effects say only one thing – they were the works from dark volitions. The suffering of those who accepted their promises as trustworthy, while they themselves had the capacity to investigate with their clarified intuitive perceptions, is only the consequence of neglect of personal duty.

The sincerity of those who today cry out for help is revealed when they are offered a way to the only thing that will help them – knowledge of the Laws of Creation so that they can navigate out of their self-created maze. Those who are sincere in their pleas will recognise the help because they will also see the strength and the purity that it contains. Others will be kept from seeing these due to the weaknesses and faults such as have been mentioned above, which they will resist getting rid of. In their response (inward and outward) to being alerted to the existence of the necessary help, will lie men's final decision, for following it would be the quickened development, growth and delivery of the fruit of this final decision – a sinking to spiritual death through disintegration, or upliftment to eternal existence and the experiencing of previously unimaginable bliss and purest joy.

Everything that has been written here has come to me through my attempt at delving into the Work – *In the Light of Truth – The Grail Message,* by Abd-ru-shin. It is made available to mankind through the authority of the Verlag Alexander Bernhardt (The Alexander Bernhardt Publishing Co.) at www.alexander-bernhardt.com. This publishing company is situated upon a settlement on a Mountain (Vomperberg) in Vomp, Austria, where the Author resided and had His home, and from where He delivered lectures of The Grail Message to willing listeners.

In the Light of Truth – The Grail Message, teaches about Creation and the Laws that govern it, in a manner that leaves no gaps, because it answers all questions that could possibly exist in the minds of men. It even goes further to include explanations about things that even a perfected human spirit in its spiritual home would still not be able to *know.*

With this work I wish to draw the attention of the reader or listener to the above-mentioned Source of the helpful Hints which alone made my expressed recognitions possible. I do so only for those who truly wish to *know,* for only they, in any case, would be willing and able to bestir themselves to see what I wish to point to with it. May God grant the strength for this!

CPSIA information can be obtained at www.ICGtesting.com
Printed in the USA
LVOW082351040212

266983LV00003B/4/P